Brett

KEVIN ALLEN has been a sportswriter for fourteen years, and has covered the NHL for *USA Today* for the past six years. He is thirty-six years old, and lives in Ypsilanti, Michigan, with his wife, three children, and a weak slap shot.

BRETT HULL AND KEVIN ALLEN

Brett

M&S

An M&S Paperback from
McClelland & Stewart Inc.
The Canadian Publishers

An M&S Paperback from McClelland & Stewart Inc.

First printing October 1992
Cloth edition printed 1991
Published by arrangement with Prentice-Hall Canada Inc.

Canadian Cataloguing in Publication Data

Hull, Brett, 1964-
Brett

"An M&S paperback."
Previously published under title: Brett: shootin' and smilin'.
ISBN 0-7710-4271-X

1. Hull, Brett, 1964- . 2. Hockey players - Canada - Biography.
I. Allen, Kevin, 1956- . II. Title.

GV848.5.H85A3 1992   796.962'092   C92-094756-5

Front cover photo: Dan Hamilton/Vantage Point Studios
Back cover photo: Canapress/Darrell Sandler
Cover design: Stephen Kenny

Unless otherwise credited, all photographs courtesy of Joanne Robinson.

Published simultaneously in the United States of America by
Firefly Books

Printed and bound in Canada

McClelland & Stewart Inc.
The Canadian Publishers
481 University Avenue
Toronto, Ontario
M5G 2E9

Contents

Dedications

To Terri, whose patience provides her husband the opportunity to be a writer. To Erin, Kelsey and Shane for bringing happiness to both of us.

Kevin Allen

To Kelly Muir and family, and Jim Toninato. I never dreamed I could have friends like you. To all my friends and critics who have helped along the way.

Brett Hull

ACKNOWLEDGEMENTS

Writing is a solitary endeavor, but a book can only be accomplished by committee. Many thanks are due. Many debts are owed. Most are too large to be repaid. Start with the other Hull children, Bobby Jr., Blake, Bart and Michelle, whose memories became the library of Brett Hull information. All gave time freely.

Add in Hall of Famer Bobby Hull, Brett's father, whose only requirement for an interview was, "make sure you let the whole world know how proud I am of Brett."

Not all memories are available on video cassette. So gratitude must go to Minnesota-Duluth coach Mike Sertich and former UMD players Bill Watson, Jim Toninato and Norm Mciver, for replaying the 1983-84 and 1985-86 Bulldogs seasons to help a bothersome writer. And to Kelly Muir for reliving the Poison years in North Vancouver.

Thanks are also due to the St. Louis Blues organization for cooperation beyond reasonable expectation: Start with president Jack Quinn for his candor and good humor about the Brett Hull contract. Move along to Jeff Trammel and Mike Caruso, who probably know my fax number by heart. Go to assistant coach Bob Berry and player Kelly Chase, who are great guys with great stories. Go next to Adam Oates, who understands Brett Hull better than anyone. And a personal note to Oatsie: I watched the replay; Brett *DID NOT* miss the break-away against your RPI team. Finally, to general manager Ron Caron for many stories over many hours. His storytelling ability is matched only by his passion for life.

Thanks also to:

Brian Burke, the Vancouver Canucks' director of hockey operations, for being in his office every day at six a.m., ready to take a reporter's phone call;

Bob Goodenow, executive director of the NHL Players' Association, for giving me time when it seemed he had none to give.

Minnesota-Duluth sports information director Bob Nygaard, Western Collegiate Hockey Association public relations director Doug Spencer, RPI sports information director Al Shibley, USA Hockey's Tom Douglis, *Hockey News*'s Rand Simon and *USA TODAY*'s Steve Ballard for providing facts and fax when they were desperately needed.

Calgary Herald sportswriter Eric Duhatschek and *Duluth News-Tribune & Herald* sportswriter Kevin Pates for providing much-needed background.

Friend Tim Robinson for continually missing *David Letterman*, to transcribe all of my tapes.

Friend and editor Dave McVety for helping fine-tune the manuscript, for the small price of hamburgers and pizza.

Penticton coach Rick Kozuback, and former players Ian Kidd and Allie Cook and others who may have contributed a story, a telephone number or a fact or two.

Special thanks are owed to those who were the glue that kept the project together. Included is Joanne Robinson, Brett's mother, a woman of extraordinary wit and talent. She rummaged in her house to find pictures and rummaged in her mind to find stories. From her heart, she gave insight into the development of the NHL's top goal scorer.

Next, there is Blues vice-president Susie Mathieu. Brett says the Blues organization would collapse if she ever left. I do know the book project would have crashed and burned without her assistance. She was was always there. Saturdays. Sundays. A.M or P.M. Susie begged, cajoled and insisted, to get people to call me. She is an amazing woman. Susie, you work too hard.

Finally, there is Greg Graessley. He is my attorney, editor, softball teammate and chief critic. He is also my closest friend. When I wanted someone to listen, he did. When I wanted an opinion, he gave. When I needed help, he came. He went with me, chapter by chapter. Having him along made it a smoother, more enjoyable journey.

And a final thanks to Brett, who allowed me to get a peek at what's behind that engaging smile.

Kevin Allen

PREFACE

Moncton, New Brunswick. It's late October 1986, and I'm in the last place I want to be with the last person I want to see.

Golden Flames coach Terry Crisp has summoned me to his office, interrupting my awesome dressing-room rendition of a Neil Young tune.

Crispy was always furious at me — but this time he blew like Mount St. Helen.

He told me he had just gotten off the phone with Calgary Flames general manager Cliff Fletcher.

"I told Cliff I want you off my team,"

he bellowed. "I told him I want you out of my town. I don't want you anywhere near my players. I don't even want you on my planet."

All I could think of to say was, "What did I do?"

There was no need for an answer, because I already knew what he hated about me. He hated that I was having fun.

Crisp climbed on my back the day I arrived at the Flames' minor-league affiliate in the American Hockey League. He had benched me, and even demoted me once to the fourth line. Daily, he ridiculed me and screamed at me. But I was still having a good time, and he couldn't figure out why.

He couldn't figure out why I grinned when I played. He couldn't figure out why I sang during practice. He couldn't figure out why I would stand at centre ice after a morning skate and fire pucks out of arena exits.

He couldn't figure out how I could be Hall of Famer Bobby Hull's son and manage to go through an entire American Hockey League season without getting into a fight.

Terry Crisp thought I was a nightmare in 1986-87. In his wildest dreams, he never could have believed I would someday win the Hart Trophy as the National Hockey League's most valuable player. He could not have dreamed I was capable of scoring eighty-six goals in one season. He would have laughed in your face if you told him that someday I would get a $7.1 million contract.

But here I am playing the game my way and having an excellent time in the NHL. True, I'm better conditioned than I was when I played in Moncton. Yet my tune hasn't changed one note since the day Crisp threatened to kick me out of his life.

It bothers me to no end when it's suggested I didn't care about hockey until the St. Louis Blues traded for me. All my life, I've been inaccurately portrayed as a guy who didn't want it badly enough. Goal scoring came so easily to me that people said, "Look at him. He's not even trying." That's absolutely wrong. Composure was continually mistaken for indifference. How do you score all the goals I have without working?

I have always worked. I worked in Penticton, British Columbia, when I scored 105 goals in 1983-84; I worked at Minnesota-Duluth when I scored 32 goals in 48 games in 1984-85 and 52 more in 42 games in 1985-86; I worked in Moncton when I netted 50 goals. And I worked when I was playing part-time in Calgary and had 26 goals in 52 games, before being traded to St. Louis in 1988.

It just so happens I have an awesome amount of fun when I play. Wayne Gretzky is the only other player I watch who seems to have as much fun as I do playing hockey. I play the way Mick Jagger sings — with passion, with improvisation, with bravado. I can't be your beast of burden, playing hockey like some well-programmed android. I get no satisfaction unless I'm enjoying myself on the ice.

Other players could be more successful if they were less uptight about the game. They concentrate on looking tough and mean, so coaches think they're intense and working hard. They forget to use their pure skills. All they need is the guts to play the way they know the game should be played. They just need to have some fun.

There was no fun in Moncton that season. I was losing it when I called my agent, Brian Burke, and told him to get me out of there.

I call him Burkie. He is a former minor league player and Harvard Law school graduate, who chews tobacco and spits out perfect common-sense advice. What I liked most about him was that he didn't pull punches.

He flew to Moncton as soon I told him I needed to talk to him.

"I can't stand it here. We've got to do something," I said.

"If I called Cliff Fletcher, what could I tell him?" Burkie asked. "That I have a pudgy, highly-paid minor-leaguer who wants out?"

He knew that wasn't the way either of us operated. Being a bellyacher wasn't my style.

We sat in my apartment for a few hours and talked it out. "Professional hockey is not a democracy," Burkie said. "Coaches don't have to solicit your opinion. Terry Crisp doesn't have to care what you think."

Burkie and I agreed that, if I stuck it out in Moncton and didn't let Terry Crisp get to me, I would eventually get a chance to show what I could do.

We were right.

CHAPTER 1

PLAYING
WITH
JETS

Not many National Hockey League players can claim the nastiest check they
ever delivered was against their mother.

It's 1969. I'm a five-year-old, trying
desperately to master skating backwards, at Oak Park Arena in suburban
Chicago. I'm chugging blindly across
the ice as fast as my chubby legs will
carry me.

My mom, Joanne, is a professional
figure skater for Hilton Hotel shows.
She's on the ice, gracefully teaching
youngsters how to avoid the choppy
skating form adopted by her third-
oldest son.

Mom had no idea of her peril, until she felt her fire-hydrant-sized offspring becoming an impact player. *Thud!* It was like Scott Stevens catching some unsuspecting Minnesota North Stars forward with his eyeball glued to the puck. Mom was launched into the air. She crash-landed on her tailbone. Bruised and dazed, she crawled off the ice.

Who says I can't hit? Dad had to lift her from the car at the doctor's office. Being carried was so painful to her backside that she insisted on crawling up the stairs.

"You should have realized then," I tell her, "that I was destined to be a pain in your butt from time to time."

My entire life, with the exception of three years in North Vancouver, has been spent around a professional hockey environment. My dad, Bobby, signed with the Chicago Blackhawks for the 1957-58 season and played there fifteen years. He married Mom in 1960, and they had five kids. Bobby Jr. was born in 1961, Blake in 1962, me in 1964, Bart in 1969 and Michelle in 1970. I was the only one without a U.S. birthplace. I was born in the Ontario city of Belleville, where my family spent the summers.

I wasn't exactly a natural at hockey, early in my career. I tried to quit teams more than once because I was cold. And sometimes, I wouldn't participate in pre-game warmups because I thought they were a waste of time.

Even after Mom taught me to skate, Dad and two teammates, Chico Maki and Phil Esposito, had to hold me down to force skates on me, at a Chicago Blackhawks Christmas party.

At four, I played on an Oak Park house league team. My skating was so wobbly that the referee carried me to the face-off circle, to prevent the game from turning into a marathon. He grew weary of that plan, and finally just let me stand in the opposition zone.

Of course, I headed straight for the net, low left wing circle. I put it in park and waited for the puck. Mom says I scored the game-winning goal from there during my first league game. That's too excellent to be true.

When my NHL career took off, reporters were always comparing me to Dad. When I'm asked about my shot, I usually say it's a product of Hull genes. Dad supposedly could shoot the puck at more than a hundred miles an hour. My brothers shoot bullets. I shoot bullets. We're the sons of a gun. That's genetics.

But one day last year, Mom, who divorced my father in 1980, said she had a beef with me.

"I keep reading that you inherited all your ability from your father," she said. "Have you forgotten that I was a professional skater? I'm the one who taught you how to skate."

"Mom," I said, "I'm actually doing you a favor by not crediting you for my skating. It's the worst part of my game."

The Hull brothers all love to shoot the puck. When Blake was hired this year to do advertising for the NHL expansion team, Tampa Bay Lightning, he was re-introduced to Tony Esposito, who is the Lightning's Director of Player Development. We knew Tony when he was a young goaltender with the Blackhawks.

"Oh, I remember you — you little punk," Esposito told Blake with a laugh. "I used to get so mad at you, I used to shoot pucks at your head."

By the time Tony came to the Blackhawks in 1969-70, Bobby Jr. and Blake already had wicked risers. But more aggravating than Blake's velocity, was his tendency to fire at will.

Tony would be talking to Dad or Hall of Fame teammate Stan Mikita, and suddenly hear one of Blake's missiles whistling past his ear. That would irritate him. One time, Tony got so mad he kept firing pucks at Blake. He missed. So he threw his gloves and stick at him.

The first people to notice I could shoot probably were those who rode the train near the outdoor rink in the Chicago suburb of Elmhurst, Illinois. At seven, I played on the Elmhurst Huskies with Tommy Stapleton, son of former Blackhawks defenseman Pat Stapleton, and Tony Granato, who now plays for the Los Angeles Kings. Granato recalls I used to line up pucks at centre ice and fire away at the trains. At that point, you could see my hockey career was on the right track.

My memories and my love of hockey began in 1971, when Dad jumped to the World Hockey Association to play for the Winnipeg Jets. I was seven when we moved to Winnipeg. Bobby Jr. was eleven; Blake was ten; Bart was only two. Michelle was a baby. We had no clue of the significance of Dad joining a rival league. We knew nothing of the $1 million signing bonus or ten-year contract, or the national publicity that came when a megastar jumped leagues. All we cared about was that we were moving to Canada, and Dad said we were going to get snowmobiles. He neglected to say a thing about Winnipeg winters.

The Hull boys, with our light hair and wild ways, were nicknamed the White Tornados in Chicago, by Blackhawks trainer Lou Varga. We lived up to our reputation in Winnipeg.

Winnipeg made a big deal about signing my dad, for good reason. The Golden Jet's presence added instant credibility to the league and the franchise. At age thirty-two, he was still among the NHL's premier players. In name recognition, he rivaled Bobby Orr. There were few before and few after who matched Dad's blend of speed, strength, shot and scoring touch. The season before, he had scored fifty goals, for the fifth time in his career.

On June 27, 1971, the Hull family was greeted by a motorcade that went from the airport to the Fort

Garry Hotel. A parade was followed by a ceremony at Winnipeg's main intersection of Portage and Main. It was Africa-hot that day, with way too many speeches for the Hull boys. Dad was at the podium, holding up a six-foot-long $1 million cheque, and promising "to do my darndest to make the WHA go."

Meanwhile, his boys were running wild behind him, as though we were leading a cattle drive.

For the next eight years, the Winnipeg Arena was my playground. The Hull boys were at the rink all the time, always in everyone's hair. Jets practices were happy hour. We were friends with anyone who would give us a stick. When the team finished practice, the Hulls would begin. We would get right in line with those staying around for extra work. Goaltenders Joe Daley and Ernie Wakely would hang around and face our shots, until they decided we'd had enough.

Defenseman Larry Hillman, a great guy, would put in practice fine-tuning his not-so-wicked slap shot — a futile exercise. Larry used a stick that was straighter than a Baptist preacher.

When Larry dribbled a shot toward the goal, Dad would yell, "Christ, Larry, my boys shoot harder than you do."

I liked to line up pucks at centre ice and try to hit that godawful, ugly portrait of Queen Elizabeth hanging on the arena wall. Dad said I could shoot like an NHL player when I was ten, but I never was good enough to nail the Queen.

Kent Nilsson, who came to the Jets in 1976-77, gave me a few lessons about shooting accuracy. They called him "Magic." After lining up ten pucks at centre ice, he would turn to Bobby Jr., Blake and me and say, "I'll bet you boys five dollars I can hit the cross bar seven times."

We would shake our heads in disbelief, and Nilsson would proceed to clang the bar eight or nine times. When he was done, he would stand there holding out his hand.

Dad wasn't one to coach his boys. His idea of teaching was to tell us to watch him. And we did. It probably helped my development as a goal scorer to watch and practice with the best professional line of the 1970s. When Ulf Nilsson and Anders Hedberg came from Sweden in 1974, it was immediately clear Hull-Nilsson-Hedberg would be an awesome line combination.

Defenseman Lars-Erik Sjoberg also came from Sweden. He was a perfect complement to the line, playing in the 1970s like Paul Coffey plays today. He lacked Coffey's speed, but he operated like a fourth forward. Sjoberg would bring the puck up ice, and give it to Nilsson. Back to Sjoberg. Over to Anders. Leave it for Dad, who would be roaring over the line. Snap shot. Top shelf. Jets goal.

Their scoring plays always looked so easy because all the work was done before the shot. Dad or Anders would usually finish the play into at a half-open net, because the goaltender had been sucked in by one or more of many passes. I remember one particular power-play goal that was amazing. There were nine passes without the opposition touching the puck, before Anders ripped it into the net.

You'll never see a guy handle the puck with more flair than Ulfie did. He could perform tricks like a circus juggler. He would lift the puck on his stick, bounce it around a while, flip it high in the air, then use his skate to kick it over his head. He would catch it on his neck like a soccer ball. It was actually quite awesome.

Ulfie was a personal favorite for Bobby Jr. and me — if only because he shot right-handed. Dad shot left-handed, so only Blake could use his sticks. In fact, Dad would get ticked when Blake didn't use his stick. When he caught Blake using Chris Bordeleau's stick he would scold him. "I've watched you play, and my stick — the weight and the curve — is perfect for your game."

That left Bobby Jr. and I to mercilessly hound Ulfie for sticks. I probably broke about fifty of Ulfie's sticks while scoring more than a hundred goals one season for the Tuxedo Jets.

There were times when we had so many of Ulfie's sticks that he had to come to us and borrow some back for games. Bobby Jr. also took Mike Ford's sticks regularly. Before each practice, Ulfie and Ford would come to the stick-cutting table on a rescue mission. They had to retrieve some sticks before we sawed all of them down to suit our needs.

The situation was so ludicrous that Bobby Jr. tried to tell Ulfie how to order his sticks.

"This stick is too whippy for me," he would tell Ulf.

"Too bad. This is my stick," Ulf would say.

Ulfie, who was constantly at our house, used to bring us Jofa equipment from Sweden every fall. But we still used to take everything but the sweater off his back.

Last year, Ulfie interviewed me for Swedish television.

"Brett, my final question to you, and I want you to be truthful," he said. "How many of my sticks did you steal in those days?"

"Hundreds," I said. "Well into the hundreds."

Late Jets trainer Bill Bozak, whose son Ryan is an NHL linesman, was probably the nicest man ever to walk this earth. Bozie treated the Hull kids like we were Jets players. Every time one of us would get hurt, Mom would call Bozie before she dialed a doctor.

Once, Blake hurt his hamstring playing football, and insisted only Bozie could treat him properly. He swears that, as soon as Bozie wrapped him, the pain disappeared.

Mom strained her back during a Jets home game, and was taken right down to see Bozie. He manipulated her bones and the pain vanished.

"He's got magic hands," Mom would joke.

Bozie never passed judgment on an injury. If you came to see him for a hangnail, he gave you the same consideration and sympathy he gave a player with a broken leg.

The Jets had a Finnish left wing named Heikki Riihiranta, who was always in the trainer's room. Before every game, Bozie would tape his wrists, then knees, then ankles, then thighs and finally his ribs. Virtually, his entire body would be covered with tape. He went in weighing 190 and left at about 210.

Curiosity got the best of me. "Just how many injuries does Heikki have?" I asked.

"Oh, he's not injured," Bozie said. "He just thinks it feels good to be taped."

The only time we really had on-ice instruction from Dad was when he and Ulfie would join us for a game at a Winnipeg outdoor rink. It was always Nilsson and Hull against the Hull kids and all of their invitees, at the Tuxedo Community Centre. I don't think we ever won a game. I don't think we ever got close to winning a game. For one thing, every time you managed to get the puck, Ulf would steal it away immediately.

Those games probably were where Bart's competitive nature became clearly established. These days, he plays fullback for the Ottawa Rough Riders of the Canadian Football League. Back then, he played hockey like a linebacker. It was impossible to make him happy in those games. If you didn't get him the puck, he was madder than a hornet. If you gave him the puck, he would be become more enraged, because he felt you were patronizing him.

In either case, he would come after you with stick raised and eyes glazed like some psycho ax murderer.

"You guys aren't trying," he'd scream, while administering a two-hander across your arm.

Bart is an exceptional athlete. At age nine, he would put his street shoes inside Jets forward Peter Sullivan's skates, after practice, and go wheeling around the ice. Even with tendon protectors flapping around the joints of his knees, he could fly around the ice.

My brothers and I always felt like we were part of the Winnipeg Jets. Bobby Jr. was the stick boy, and the rest of us helped out in the dressing room. We could always sit at the end of the bench during games.

The most awesome professional game I ever saw was the Jets' exhibition game against the Soviet National Team in January, 1978.

Dad always got pumped to play the Soviets, maybe because he had been snubbed for the Summit Series in 1972, after his defection to the WHA. In 1975, Dad played well — scoring six goals during the first four games — in the Summit II series, pitting WHA All-Stars against the Soviets.

In 1978, he still had a fire for international competition. The Jets played a three-game exhibition series against the Soviet National Team in Tokyo — the Soviets won all three — then returned to Winnipeg for a game.

Apparently, Dad was hell-bent on making sure the Jets had a better effort in front of the Jets fans. Bobby Jr., who was in the dressing room right before the game, told me Dad addressed the team before it went out on the ice. Dad coached even when he wasn't the coach. This night he gave specific orders to everyone.

One by one, each Jets line was assigned a Soviet line to check. Each time, Dad would say, "We need your line to check. Your only job is preventing them from scoring."

When he was done with those assignments, a grin spread across his face. "And while you guys are doing all that checking, Ulf, Anders and I will get all the goals we need."

The game went according to Dad's plan: Jets 5, Soviets 3. Bobby Hull scored three times and assisted on one of Ulfie's two goals.

Jets fans were on their feet from the opening whistle until Dad scored with eight seconds remaining, to clinch the victory. Dad's line, matched up against the Soviets' top line of Valeri Kharlamov, Vladimir Petrov and Boris Mikhilov, outscored them 5-0.

Another highlight for us came in 1974-75, when Dad broke Phil Esposito's record of seventy-six goals in a season. He scored one in each of the final two games to do it.

Goal Number Seventy-Six was the most difficult. He double-shifted the whole game, and even moved to the point once or twice. But he didn't score until the final twenty seconds of a 9-5 loss to Quebec. He scored on his eighteenth shot of the game, against goaltender Richard Brodeur.

The record-breaker was less dramatic, coming in the second period of a 5-5 tie against San Diego. Anders Hedberg fed him a backhand pass, and Dad buried a wrist shot.

I remember reading that late Toronto Maple Leafs owner Harold Ballard refused to allow Dad's accomplishment to be posted on Toronto's scoreboard. I was ten. I thought Ballard was a jerk.

On February 14, 1975, Bobby Hull scored three goals against Houston goaltender Ron Graham, to become the first player since NHL Hall of Famer Maurice "Rocket" Richard to score fifty goals in fifty games. He didn't get much recognition for that either, because it had been accomplished in the WHA, and not the NHL. I would remember all this fifteen years later, when I was offered a lucrative contract by a fledgling league.

The Jets' first league championship came in 1975-76, when they defeated Gordie Howe's Houston Aeros in four straight games. They wrapped it up with a 9-1 win in Winnipeg. It was bedlam. We were all on the ice, jumping around. It was the Hull kids who prevented a lot of equipment from being taken by the fans. We picked up all the gloves and sticks and threw them into the bench. It was almost as though we had helped win it.

The funniest thing I saw in my days in Winnipeg was when Dad's famous hairpiece was yanked from his head, during a game against the Birmingham Bulls. You have to understand that Dad and his hairpiece were inseparable. He wore it on and off the ice. He went into the corner with a full crop, and he came out bald. I think it was Dave Hanson who ended up with my dad's rug in his hand.

Dad was furious. But he wasn't vain enough to let it affect his play. He went to the dressing room, donned a helmet and returned to score two goals.

He got a standing ovation from the crowd.

Bobby Jr. was away playing junior hockey by then. I was still laughing the next night, when I called to tell him the story.

We were always causing a stir — even away from the rink. Japanese manufacturer Suzuki gave my dad two snowmobiles when he signed with Winnipeg, and we went crazy on them. We'd tie ropes on the snowmobiles and ski behind them, out on a ranch that Dad had bought in nearby Vivian. We were probably lucky we didn't get killed.

Out there, we could ride forever. Often, we would ride two miles down to the Springfield Hutterite religious community for their communal lunch. They knew Dad, and fed us until we were ready to burst. One thing a Hull can do, besides shoot, is eat. "Brett, when you and I eat, we take no prisoners," Bobby Jr. said.

When the WHA playoffs were over, the Winnipeg Arena kept its ice for a while. One year, Bobby Jr., Blake and I invited our friends to the arena for a scrimmage game. The arena was dark when we arrived with Dad, who went upstairs to talk to Jets officials.

Bart was the only one who knew how to turn on the lights. He went straight for the switches. For all we knew or cared, throwing those switches cost the Jets $2,000.

We had about fifteen players — including two goaltenders in full gear — and we had played for about fifteen minutes, when Stan, the arena manager, arrived in a rage. Dad was occasionally at odds with Stan over the ice conditions.

Because Dad could skate like an express train, he liked his ice hard. Sometimes Stan would have too much water on it to suit Dad. "If he waters it one more time, I'm going to go down there and cut his hose into tiny pieces," Dad would say.

Stan was in a snit when he spotted the Hull boys having a good time on the ice at the Jets' expense.

"You kids get off the ice," he bellowed. "Get out of here."

He stormed off, and turned off the arena lights.

We waited fifteen minutes before Bobby Jr. sent Bart again to flip the switches.

Stan came out again, huffing. "I told you kids to get out of here, now."

Suddenly, from high in the stands, came this husky voice. It boomed like the voice of God.

"Stan-lee," he shouted, "those are my boys, and you leave them alone. They can play on that ice."

"Oh, yes sir, Bobby," Stan said. "Just make sure they turn off the lights."

Stan was muttering under his breath when he left. We played about four hours of hockey. It may have been the best four hours of hockey any group of boys ever played — and we probably didn't remember to turn off the lights.

Not long after that, my parents split up. My mom, Blake, Michelle and I flew to Vancouver on a Winnipeg jet, in 1979. Bobby Jr. went off to play hockey in Lethbridge, Alberta. Blake would soon head off to Cornwall, Ontario, to play. Dad stayed in Winnipeg. Mom and Dad were officially divorced in 1980. We were scattered throughout Canada.

It would be ten years, at Bobby Jr.'s wedding, before all the kids were together again.

CHAPTER 2

THE

POISON

YEARS

At age seventeen, Wayne Gretzky and Mario Lemieux were already headed for greatness. At age seventeen, I was headed for donuts.

As an adolescent, I was a better candidate for Weight Watchers than the National Hockey League. Fat chance anyone expected me to end up a $1-million-per-year hockey player. People saw me as a pudgy, fun-loving, music-crazed bum, cruising North Vancouver in a deathtrap 1975 Pinto station wagon.

I was playing Midget hockey in North Vancouver, weighing between 210 and 215 pounds — about ten to fifteen pounds heavier than my NHL playing weight. I didn't lead the team in scoring. I wasn't even the Number One right wing. It wasn't surprising when no junior team showed the slightest interest in Vancouver's only right wing who came with love handles. At that point in my life, any thoughts about the NHL were merely fantasy.

My reality was partying with friends, playing high-school and recreational sports, listening to music and leaving the world wondering just what the heck I was going to do with my life.

My home life had changed considerably. Mom met an accountant named Harry Robinson, and they were married in 1982. I was Harry's best man at the wedding. By this time, Blake had already left. Only Bart, Michelle and I lived with Mom and Harry in the Vancouver suburbs.

Mom and Harry probably were the only two adults in the Vancouver area who believed I might turn out all right. Even their faith was shaken from time to time.

After I had been sentenced to summer school for the second time, for failing English, Mom just shook her head.

"I know we are going to see you get your diploma," she said, "but I think you and I both are going to have long grey beards when you do. They'll have to push us both down the aisle in wheelchairs."

Maybe I didn't know what I was going to do in the future, but I was having an excellent time in the present, running amok with my best friend, Kelly Muir, whose passion for mischief matched my own. We hatched one harebrained scheme after another.

Once, we heard about a possible beer strike, and decided to strike it rich by cornering the local beer market. We convinced someone to buy as much as we could afford. I borrowed $138 from my stepfather, and cases were stacked floor to ceiling in my bedroom. The plan was to sell them for a tasty profit to Vancouver's parched masses.

The problem was, the strike didn't last. Our entrepreneurial dreams dashed, we consoled ourselves with liquidation of inventory.

"The only thing that bothered me about that deal," Harry said later, "was that you didn't even give me a beer."

On my nineteenth birthday, a group of us went to a David Bowie concert at B.C. Stadium in downtown Vancouver. We wanted to sneak in something to drink, so I loaded up a wine flask and stuffed it inside my Canterbury rugby pants. There was a football-sized bulge running up my inseam to my crotch.

"Do you think they'll let me in?" I asked.

"You look like you have elephantitis of the testicles," Kelly cracked. "Other than that, I think you'll have no problem."

We got in, and somehow I became separated from everyone. In a crowd of about 60,000 in B.C. Stadium there was absolutely no chance we would meet on the way out. I walked for about fifteen minutes before I spied Kelly and the group running toward me.

"How did you find me?"

"Christ," Kelly said. "We could hear you singing Bowie songs three blocks away."

Thus began my singing legend. I'm an awesome singer, or at least a very distinctive one.

Kelly and I were a wild mix. Mom worked at keeping our shenanigans to a minimum.

One Sunday, we came to my house very late and headed straight to the refrigerator for our weekly assault on the leftover roast beef. Mom always made three roasts — one for dinner, and two for sandwiches. We committed two sins that evening. First, we created an unprecedented mess, even by our shabby standards. Second, we made more noise than the fans at Chicago Stadium. Our doom was assured when we woke Mom and Harry.

Kelly and I had just plopped on my bed when Mom came downstairs and found our trail of destruction. Her look that night would have backed-down Bob Probert. She was breathing fire, as she ordered Kelly out of both her house and her life.

Kelly was so shaken by Mom's fury that he didn't even think to get dressed. He walked the four blocks home in his underwear. She yelled at me so loudly that Kelly swears he heard her at his house. We deserved it. We always deserved it.

Mom's face was the color of rare roast beef during that episode, but she was madder still on one other occasion. She had a major meltdown the evening she came home to discover Kelly and I having a baby-powder fight in the basement. There was dust everywhere. I almost got exiled to Winnipeg for that one.

While still under age, Kelly grew all the facial hair he could manage in a week, and drove across the border to the state of Washington. He went to several beer stores, before finding one that didn't ask for identification.

On the way back across the border, the customs agent eyed him suspiciously.

"Do you have any beer or alcohol to declare," he asked.

"How can I?" Kelly said, with the most angelic face he'd ever had in his life. "I'm under age."

The officer waved the car on, failing to notice, as it drove away, that the bumper was dragging on the road from the weight of the beer filling the trunk.

Our fun generally evolved from horseplay more than anything criminal. We were much too smart to get into any real trouble, although our teachers probably never would have never guessed that. I left college with a reasonable 2.7 grade-point average, but at Carson Graham High School in North Vancouver, I never got a grade higher than a *C*, except in gym. Kelly and I majored in absenteeism, with a minor in mischief.

What I loved about Mom was that she trusted me. She would try to rein me in on occasion, and of course I would be too stubborn to listen, but I think she always knew in her heart I was never headed for any serious trouble. We were friends. We'd wrestle around in the living room. She called it Mother Crusher vs. Brother Crusher. Bart and Michelle thought it was great fun.

I think we were friends even when I moved out of the house after a big fight, when I was seventeen. I moved over to Kelly's house.

I remember she called me. "I'll bet living with Kelly isn't as much fun as living at home," she said.

"Oh yes, it is."

"I'll bet Mrs. Muir doesn't cook as well as I do."

"Oh yes, she does."

We both started laughing. Mom knew I was only putting up a front. Another thing I inherited from my dad, besides a slap shot, was his pigheadedness. I always think I'm right.

Another of my North Vancouver adventures involved a certain degree of irony. On graduation night, several of the guys, including me, slept on the lawn at Connie Quinn's home. Her father was Jack Quinn, president of the Vancouver Canadians baseball team of the Pacific Coast League.

Quinn is now president of the St. Louis Blues. He was aware his daughter knew me, but only recently discovered I had slept on his property. Connie kept insisting her dad might even have seen me, but Quinn had no recollection.

"You might have even seen him on my graduation night. Remember we rented a Winnebago, and the girls slept inside and guys on the lawn?"

"Well, what time did Brett get to our house?"

"Oh, about 3:30 or 4:00 o'clock in the morning."

That was about my normal arrival time for such occasions.

"Geez, I'm sorry I missed Brett," Quinn said. "But I don't think he had any regrets."

Skipping classes was my only problem in school. For me, hearing an excellent tune on the radio was a valid enough reason to ditch. Station CFOX in Vancouver — the Electric Lunch, with awesome music from the '60s and '70s — was our guiding light. We'd spend hours listening to music and playing our own version of *Name That Tune.*

As the music began, we raced to see who could name title and artist the quickest. Because Kelly was a drummer he generally could pick up the beat faster. But if we played today, I'd kick his butt. I know the lyrics of every decent song ever recorded. That means my repertoire covers tunes before 1976. Anything recorded after 1975 is awful.

"I was born too late," I used to tell Kelly. "I should have been a teen-ager in the 1960s. My fantasy would have been to be at Woodstock."

In Vancouver, I'm probably best known for my chocolate-brown '75 Pinto station wagon. The car was more notorious than my slap shot. Mom and Harry bought it for Blake, and I inherited it when he went off to play Junior A hockey in Cornwall. Blake called it the "Poison Pinto," and my friends shortened it to simply "Poison."

Poison was a beast. Rust held it together. The car never met a vacuum. Rank-smelling clothes, McDonald's wrappers and cans were everywhere. You needed delousing if you spent any time in Poison.

Mom thought it was a great car for her kids, because its top speed was about forty-five miles per hour. There was no chance any of us would be killed, drag racing in Poison down Vancouver's streets. Poison had the acceleration of a Zamboni. You could beat Poison off a light with a twenty-six-inch Schwinn bicycle. Poison would only make it up a hill in first gear with the gas pedal pushed to floor. The unofficial record for most occupants in Poison at one time was nine — six guys and three girls. We did have to drop off a few folks at the bottom of one hill to insure we could get to the top. It wasn't really an inconvenience. It just meant we had to make two trips up some hills to get everyone to the top.

The police once got Mom and Harry out of bed at four a.m. because Poison was found parked in the middle of our street. The cops thought the thief had abandoned Poison after realizing he had just stolen the worst car known to Western Civilization. My theory is that he was overcome by the smell and crawled away to die in some alley.

Most of my friends either rode in, or drove, Poison at one time or another. Once, while I was playing junior hockey in Penticton, Mom called to tell me that Poison had been stolen while she was on holiday. She had already called the police and filled out the reports.

A few days later, I had the unfortunate duty of informing Mom that I had solved the case.

"Mom, cancel the all-points-bulletin on my car."

"You found it?"

"Not exactly. It kind of drove into my driveway, up here in Penticton."

"It certainly didn't do that by itself."

"No. My friends, Deena Robertson, Monique Davidson, Shelly Marsh and Rhonda Holden, borrowed the car to come up here to see me."

Mom didn't think the story was quite as funny as I did. She wasn't comfortable knowing Poison's ignition was so worn that absolutely any automobile key would fire it up. Blake's friends would take it for a late-night ride on the town. They would come rolling in loudly before the sun came up, then run like crazy for fear Mom and Harry would catch them. Deena, Monique, Shelly Marsh and Rhonda were the first group whose joy ride lasted past dawn.

We used to play *Starsky and Hutch* in Poison, rolling over the hood and running over the body. We beat that car mercilessly. Still, it refused to die.

One night, Blake and I and were driving Poison down West Van Beach when the police pulled us over. This was hardly a surprise. Every officer in Vancouver recognized Poison and knew that the dome lamp was the only light in the car that worked consistently.

The window crank didn't work, so Blake had to push down the window with his hand as the officer reached the driver's side door.

"When are you Hull boys going to junk this and get a real car?" the officer said.

"We just got it fixed," Blake lied.

"Do you know your brake lights aren't working?"

"Geez, we just had 'em worked on. There must be a short in the system."

"Do you realize you only have one headlight?"

"Aw, geez, we just replaced that one a couple days ago."

"Is your turn signal burned out?"

"It just started sticking this morning."

"And what about your muffler?"

"We're planning to fix that tomorrow."

The officer just laughed. Poison was such a sorry excuse for a car that it wasn't even worth the the time it took to write the ticket. We got our zillionth warning to get Poison fixed, and went on our way.

Sports was life for Kelly and me in North Vancouver. We met on a baseball diamond. Kelly had a knee operation, and I played first base while he was recovering. He stopped by to remind me that I would be going back to third when he was ready to play.

In football, Kelly played linebacker, and I was a two-way starter on the line. Yes, Mr. Non-Intensity tried to use his body to wallop human beings — if only Terry Crisp could have seen me. I had no idea what I was doing, but I wasn't bad. Unfortunately, my most devastating hit occurred during a practice. Bob Sigmund, our star running back, met the Incredible Hull at the line of scrimmage and blew out his knee. Sorry about that.

Baseball was more my game. I have no idea what kind of statistics I had, but it's fair to say I wasn't a bunter. There was a field behind Balmoral Junior High School, and the goal of every power hitter was to hit a softball into the tennis court. I could hit a softball *over* the tennis court and onto the roof of the school. Kelly, hardly an expert on such matters, figured it was 350 feet. Actually, I thought it was a better shot when I hit it through a classroom window while school was in session.

Some say I was better at baseball than hockey when I was younger. But major league scouts don't exactly flock to Vancouver to find the next José Canseco. We didn't even have high school baseball in Vancouver.

If they had come, they wouldn't have been dazzled by my speed. One day, our coach got this brainy idea to time us around the base paths, so he could factor that into his decision-making about a batting order. Needless to say, I thought this was the worst idea I had ever heard. Our best guys were going around in fourteen or fifteen seconds, and I waddled around in twenty-four seconds. When I think something is a bad idea, I rebel.

"I could have timed you with a calendar," Coach said, or words to that effect.

What else do I remember about baseball? I recall I had front-row tickets to ZZ Top, and gave them up to play in the provincial baseball championships. That's true commitment, for a rock-and-roller like myself.

For the most part, I got along with coaches in high school. But I did have one problem with a gym teacher.

We used to play floor hockey, and he never appreciated the way I played the game or shot the puck.

One day when he grabbed me during a game, words were exchanged.

A few days later we played again, and I had the puck in my zone. Kelly liked to play goalie against me so, when I got the puck, players would clear away like the parting of the Red Sea to give me a chance to rocket a screamer at Kelly. I was winding up when the teacher came running into the game to play defense.

"Don't move away and let him shoot it," he commanded, just as I let the shot fly.

It hit the blade of his stick, deflected up, and struck him flush in the eye. This was the first, and only, time I ever saw a grown man cry.

Driving my little brother Bart crazy was another of my pastimes. We played basketball every Saturday and Sunday at Holy Trinity school. Bart and his friend, Bill Kelly, played against Kelly Muir and me on a court with eight-foot baskets. We thought we were the kings of dunk.

We played to win and, as the big brother, I made the rules without ever telling him what they were.

Rule No. 1: Every move Bart made was a foul.

Rule No. 2: Every move I made wasn't a foul.

Bart, an excellent athlete, was foolishly always looking to dunk over his brother. I was simply looking to dunk my little brother. Defense, as you might guess, wasn't my specialty. So I would just stick my knee out, and he would run right into it. He would leave every game with a charley-horse. He would also leave every game crying or swearing; usually both. It was such an excellent time.

It's funny when I think of all the times coaches said I never worked to improve. All I ever did when I was kid was play sports. In summer, I would shoot pucks three hours a day at Kelly. Maybe I didn't work at the parts of the game they wanted me to play, but I surely worked at the game I wanted to play. I worked at being a scorer. And, as far as I know, you still win games by scoring more than the other team.

Kelly and I were primarily bums in those days. We would work only when we had to, making money now and then working in Kelly's father's print shop, just enough to buy concert tickets. We'd skip classes in the morning, then a bunch of my friends would come to my house for lunch every day. Mom and Harry would be at work.

These fun times produced fond memories for many. Just last year, Monique Davidson saw Harry in Vancouver. "I never did thank you for all the lunches we had at your houses during high school," Monique said.

"What lunches?" Harry asked.

Harry and Mom had no idea that the gang used to eat at our house every day. I guess Mom figured it was just that her fat son was eating thirty-five roast beef sandwiches a week.

About this time, I was starting to wonder where I might be headed in my life. The only career I ever thought about, besides hockey, was an advertising director — sort of like the television character Darren Stevens, on *Bewitched.*

At the time, my hockey career was dying slowly in the North Van Rec Juvenile league. I only played there because my friends were playing and I was meeting them afterward, anyway. For me, hockey was reaching a dead end.

One evening, on the way home from a party, Kelly and I stopped at a park behind Balmoral school. We were talking about playing juvenile hockey that fall, and probably swapping lies about girls we knew. The conversation turned uncharacteristically serious for the two of us.

"What do you want to do with your life?" Kelly asked.

"I think I want to play pro hockey."

"You can do it," Kelly said. "The Hull name alone would get you in the door."

"It didn't do much for my brothers. They didn't make the NHL."

"Then do it with your talent. You have enough of that. Maybe it's time for you to put your nose to the grindstone."

That's for sure, I realized.

CHAPTER 3

WIGGLY, WIGGLY WOE

The Penticton Knights didn't want me in the fall of 1982; they wanted Allie Cook.

While I was coasting through the season for the North Van Rec Juvenile team, Allie was a hundred-point centre for the North Shore Winter Club Midgets. Allie and I were good friends, having played the previous year together on the midget squad.

Knights coach Rick Kozuback was selling Allie on the idea that he would be showcased for many American college recruiters, who regularly handed out scholarships to top players in the British Columbia Junior Hockey

League. He was introduced to the media as one of the Knights' top recruits.

In August, Allie called me from Penticton, where he was working at the team's hockey school. He said he had convinced coach Rick Kozuback to let me try out for the Knights. Peter "Gus" Gustafson, another one of our buddies, also got an invitation.

I said I would think about it — but I knew what my answer was going to be. First, moving five hours northeast of Vancouver, to the interior of B.C., on a longshot hope to prolong my career, wasn't very enticing. Moreover, I wasn't stupid. It was clear Kozuback only invited Gus and me because he was trying to satisfy the wants of his prized recruit, Allie. Finally, I figured they were just using the Hull name for publicity's sake.

I called Allie the next day.

"Thanks for the invitation, Allie, but I'm going to pass."

A few hours later — after I had a long discussion with Mom — Allie got another call.

"Allie, this is Brett's mom, Joanne Robinson. I just want to let you know that Brett will be going to Penticton with you."

There you have it. Brett Hull scores in Penticton, assist to Allie Cook and Joanne Hull Robinson. Mom said she wasn't going to let me give up on hockey when it was obvious I still wanted to play. She was right.

The Knights' tryout was a cattle call. There were 306 players in training camp, and I arrived weighing 226 pounds. That isn't a misprint. Neither the roster size, nor the Hull size, is exaggerated. The only guy there who outweighed me was Ian Kidd, who played briefly for the Vancouver Canucks. He weighed in at 227, and unlike me, he used his pounds to pulverize people.

If my name was Brett Smith or Brett Jones, I never would have made the Penticton Knights that season. They assigned me Dad's Number 9 without even asking if I wanted it. It was obvious they were keeping me around because my name was Hull. In fact, they more or less told me that. One of their marketing strategies was to tell fans they had a chance to watch Bobby Hull's son play.

"You're the twentieth player on the team," Kozuback told me bluntly. "You've got a lot of work to do. You've got to get in better shape, but we're willing to try it."

In their way of thinking, it would be a bonus if it turned out I could really play.

It turned out to be a bonus, and them some. With Kozuback pushing me hard to get in shape, I scored forty-eight goals in my first season in Penticton, with most of those goals coming in the second half of the season. I was the Knights' rookie of the year.

The BCJHL isn't the kind of league that normally surrenders that many goals to first-year players. For a Tier II league, it routinely acquires a fair share of B.C.'s top young players. Those who want to join Junior A teams sometimes start in the BCJHL. Also, players can participate in Tier II without jeopardizing their college eligibility.

Penticton was an attractive place to play. It's a beautiful resort town, sitting on Okanagan Lake, which is eighty miles long. The Knights' history included players who went on to the NHL, such as the Boston Bruins' Andy Moog and the New York Islanders' Ray Ferraro. The Edmonton Oilers' Joe Murphy, who was the Numbeer One pick in the 1986 National Hockey League draft, played for the Knights the season after me. Boston Bruins minor-leaguer Norm Foster was Penticton's goaltender during my first year.

In my two years at Penticton, the league's goaltenders included Darryl Reaugh, who now plays for Hartford, and Mark Fitzpatrick, who plays for the Islanders.

When I arrived in Penticton, I wasn't a typical Knights recruit. I was eighteen, and had yet to apply myself in school. They preferred sixteen- and seventeen-year-old players with good grades, who had their eyes on college scholarships. Kozuback had a well-deserved reputation for running a program that prepared players for college hockey. He worked at getting scholarships for his players and putting them in the right schools for their talent and academic needs. Recruiters, respecting Kozuback's record, flocked to our games. In my second year with the Knights, fourteen of our twenty players received scholarship offers from U.S. colleges.

My attitude about school changed in Penticton. Realizing I could earn a college scholarship, I started to work harder on my grades. Doing well in school was more important to the players in Penticton than it had been with my friends back home. I started doing my homework on the team bus. Accounting. English. Math. My grades improved. I remember taking an interior design class: I had to finish a needle-point design, so I brought it on the bus to work on it. The guys hooted on me for that, but I knew it was the only way I could get it done. The *A* was worth the grief.

Interestingly enough, Gustafson also made the team. Allie, of course, was on the team before the try-out. The three of us, who had clowned around during high school, were reunited in Penticton.

Gus, by the way, was the victim of the best practical joke I every pulled. It happened at Salt Spring, an island off the coast of British Columbia. Allie's folks owned a resort there, and he regularly invited friends to visit him.

One time, Gus brought his girlfriend with him. The three of us were sitting around telling stories, until Gus went to the store. During his absence, his girlfriend and I conspired to create a devilish prank.

When he returned, he found his friend and girl-friend in the midst of a passionate embrace. It appeared we were kissing, though in fact we're just hugging and trying desperately not to giggle.

He bolted out the door and slammed a bottle against a tree. I followed him out the door, and it took me nearly an hour to convince him that he had just witnessed the best acting performance in a love scene since Bogie and Bacall. I'll never forget the expression on his face. We still laugh about that.

The irony of the 1982-83 season was that I survived with the Knights, and Allie didn't. By midseason, he had a dispute with Kozuback and ended up playing for another team. He did get his scholarship to play at Michigan Tech. Gus also was released after about six weeks of the season.

My teammates probably remember me for my dress as much as my slap shot, during those two seasons. Guys teased me because I owned one tie that I kept tied all the time. This allowed me to just slip it on when I went on a road trip. I wore the same blue jeans time and again, and I had these dress sandals that drove Kozuback crazy. After it became clear I was going to stay, Mom bought me some clothes, including an expensive pair of Western boots. But I had an image to maintain. The first time I wore them into the dressing room, I had one pant leg tucked in, the other hanging out.

"Hullie, you are the worst dresser I've ever seen," Kozuback said, without fear of contradiction.

The Knights practiced at six a.m., and I would literally roll out of bed and head to the rink. A few times I showed up at the dressing room wearing robe and slippers.

The following season Murphy was the big star of the Penticton Knights. I heard he used to show up at those dawn practices in his robe and slippers. Tradition is very important in hockey.

Forgetfulness also marked my days in Penticton. Once, while sitting on the team bus en route to a game against the Cowichian Valley Capitals, I remembered leaving my skates back at the hotel. Foster said his parents hadn't left the hotel yet. We stopped the bus, so he could call them. Thankfully, they agreed to retrieve my skates.

Kozuback wasn't very happy about the situation. Even after the Fosters brought my skates during the second period, he didn't apparently have any intention of playing me.

But after the second period, the score was tied 4-4. Since it was a game we should have been winning, Kozuback told me to get dressed.

I scored three goals in the third period. We won 10-4.

We were one of the few teams to use higher-grade sticks — which then sold for about $105 a dozen. I broke so many that Kozuback switched in the following season to aluminum shafts.

"We're going to go broke if we don't get you away from the wood," Kozuback said.

When I snapped the fifty-dollar aluminum shaft for the first time, the guys on the team couldn't believe it.

Despite all the hullabaloo about my slap shot, my favorite move that season involved my backhand. I would skate down the right, cut across the goal crease, and wait until the goaltender dove for me. Then backhand. Top shelf. Knights' goal.

At the end of that season, Kozuback called me to discuss my future. He said if I had another strong season, then it was a certainty I would get a scholarship offer. But neither one of us had any idea how well I would play during the 1983-84 season.

By Christmas that season, I had already scored fifty goals. Everyone knew then that this wasn't going to be an ordinary season.

Broadcaster Rich Hopson, of Penticton radio station CKOK, developed a slogan for my pursuit of the league scoring record. "Hull is going for 84 in '84," Rich would say, after I scored another.

The league record was eighty-three goals, by New Westminster Royals' centre Cliff Ronning, who now plays for the Vancouver Canucks. Kozuback predicted to his friends that I would score a hundred.

I scored 105 in 56 games.

The publicity build-up for my march to a hundred goals wasn't like the world watching Roger Maris's quest to hit sixty-one home runs. But by BCJHL standards, my feats were drawing considerable attention. Out-of-town papers were sending writers, and the Vancouver papers started showing some interest. It was almost anti-climactic when I broke Ronning's record.

As it turned out I was a far better goal scorer than I was a drawing card. The Knights, who originally kept me because they thought my name would sell tickets, were rather disappointed. Fans might pay thirty dollars or more to watch me play in the NHL, but they wouldn't pay four dollars in Penticton. In an arena holding 2,000, we averaged about 875. Even during my 105-goal season, we never had a sellout.

At the All-Star break, I was named Interior Division MVP. That's only interesting because the Coastal Division MVP was Steve Tuttle, who plays with me now on the St. Louis Blues.

It was an amazing season. Scott Carter, now a part-time scout for the Vancouver Canucks, was the team's director of player personnel and statistician. He figured out that I shot the puck 614 times that season and hit the net 403 times, for a 65.6 % shooting accuracy. I scored on 26.1 % of the shots on goal, which was the team's second-best scoring percentage. No one else even attempted three hundred shots that season. If anyone ever complained about how much I shot the puck, I had a stock answer: "It's difficult to score without shooting the puck."

We had five other players with thirty or more goals — Kidd, Aaron Scott, Murray Winnicki, Rob Poindexter, Rob Schluter -- and finished the season with a 47-13 record. My good friend, Mark Verigin, with whom I enjoyed many crazy adventures, had seventeen goals in just twenty-seven games played. He was our alternate captain when he injured his eye in a game. Kozubak had the *A* put on my sweater. Mark never got it back. I've always felt kind of bad about that.

The Knights were a brash bunch that season. we weren't shy about letting people know we were good. After we beat a team on the road, the team bus stopped near the windows of the home dressing room.

Our windows would be rolled down, and a team leader would stand up and lead the Knights in our traditional victory chant. The leader would shout the verse first, and players would repeat in kind.

Eidee, Eidee, Eidee, Oh
Wiggly, Wiggly, Wiggly Woe.
Raise your hands up to the sky
The Penticton Knights have passed you by.

I don't have to tell you which team leader led that chant. Do I?

Despite winning, Kozuback remained tough — always pushing us to improve. When he wasn't looking, I would do an impersonation of him, and always end with, "And if you guys don't play better, I'm going to demote you all to Cheboygan."

No one had any idea where Cheboygan was — but it certainly sounded like somewhere we didn't want to be.

Kozuback did send a player to Alberta — actually he traded him to a team in the Alberta Junior League — to acquire a centre named Rob Schluter from St. Albert.

Schluter played in the BCJHL, and then he transferred to the Alberta league. He talked about coming back to B.C., and Kozuback heard he was probably going to Summerland — one of our archrivals. Schluter was a good playmaker, so Kozuback traded a defenseman named Darryl Olson to get him. Interleague trades weren't exactly ordinary occurrences, but Kozuback wasn't an ordinary coach.

I had played the first part of the season with Poindexter, but he was injured, and Kozy put me with Schluter. In the second half of the season, we were unstoppable. I ended the season with Tim Comeau as my left wing. He was the grinder on the line, and Schluter was the playmaker. Schluter always seemed to find me with his passes.

In the final fifteen games of the season, I had forty-three goals and thirty assists. During that period, Schluter had fifteen goals and twenty-seven assists. Six of those goals came during one game against Revelstoke. That team decided to shadow me at the expense of leaving everyone else unguarded. I assisted on all six of them.

By the end of the season, I had the 105 goals, plus 83 assists, to break the league points record of

183 set by John Newberry of Naniamo in 1979-80. He ended up playing briefly for the Montreal Canadiens.

One more amusing note is that I ended up the season playing defense in the BC Junior Final against Langley. The team was short on bodies because of five shoulder separations, plus Langley was trying to shadow me. So Kozuback decided to move both Kidd and me from right wing to defense. I remember the two of us sitting back there before one face-off. Kidd yelled over at me, laughing, "What are we doing back here?"

The joke was on Kidd, because he played so well back there that the move became permanent. He played briefly with the Vancouver Canucks, and played last season for the Milwaukee Admirals of the International Hockey League.

Kidder beat longer odds than me to make the Knights in 1982-83. He came up from Portland, Oregon, burdened by too much weight and too little talent — or so everyone thought.

Coaches weren't going to include him in their first cut to forty. There was one final intrasquad game yet to be played, and coaches were so sure of the roster they only left two guys to watch. Kidder fought three times in one period and basically set the tone for the game. One of the coaches said, "He's got heart, why don't we keep him as fortieth player," or so the story goes.

By the time, he left the BCJHL, he had set a scoring record for a defenseman previously held by Doug Lidster, who now plays for the Vancouver Canucks.

Kidder literally fought his way to the top. During his first season, he didn't win many fights but he backed down from no one. In his second season, he injured three opponents on one shift with his body-checking — two separated shoulders and a broken collarbone. His teammates tagged him "Kamikaze" after that.

He was as excited to be playing in the BCJHL as anyone I've ever met. One time, he scored a short-handed game-winner, in overtime no less. When he went on the post-game radio show, he just couldn't contain himself. "I want to thank, Ma, Pa and apple pie," he blurted out.

No one could figure out what apple pie had to do with it — other than maybe he had eaten a lot it. Kidder was a big guy.

It still didn't come easily for him. After two years in Penticton, he was only offered a partial scholarship at the University of Alaska. He was ready to quit, but team owner Larry Lund said if he would come back, he would guarantee him a college education. If he didn't get a scholarship, Lund was going to pay for it.

That was the season Kidd scored 36 goals and 105 points. In the BCJHL championship game, he was cut on the eyelid. They stitched it up without anaesthetic, and Kidd went back to the bench. North Dakota gave him a scholarship, and he helped the school win an NCAA title.

He signed a decent contract with the Canucks that included a nice signing bonus of $155,000. That was a larger signing bonus than I got on my first contract. His last deal was a minor-league contract with the Admirals — but Kidder is far from bitter. The junior longshot made it all the way to the NHL.

"At least I fooled them for a couple of years," Kidder said, with a laugh.

Another strange thing about that season was that it seemed like every team in the NHL came to look at me — except the Calgary Flames. For whatever reason, the Flames didn't get around to seeing me until the last weekend, when scout Jack Ferreira showed up.

He must have liked what he saw, because the Flames drafted me in the sixth round. I remember I wasn't all that excited about being drafted by the Flames. That was probably an omen.

Being recruited by colleges was more exciting than being drafted. It was nice to be wanted for my talent, instead of my surname. My two years in Pentiction had changed my outlook about hockey. I started to believe I had a future in the game, and if I didn't play professional hockey, I knew college would give me a life outside of sports.

Colorado College, Northern Michigan, North Dakota and Minnesota-Duluth were the colleges recruiting me with the most vigor. Michigan State approached me early in the season, then lost interest because Spartans coaches didn't believe my skating was strong enough. Kozubak, always looking to send his players to the best, asked me to give strong consideration to North Dakota. Coach Gino Gasparini's North Dakota program was impressive — but Minnesota-Duluth was the clear favorite from the beginning.

There were many reasons. The Bulldogs called first and most often. Also, UMD assistant coach Tim McDonald's low-key recruitment pitch appealed to me right away. He sold me on the idea that UMD, even though it had a roster of talented players, could find room for me to play immediately. The Bulldogs were nationally-ranked that season and advanced to the NCAA final, before losing in four overtimes to Bowling Green. Ironically, Bowling Green's overtime scoring hero was Gino Cavallini. Five years later, he and I would play on the same team in St. Louis.

The small-town side of Minnesota-Duluth also hooked me. I knew I would be comfortable there.

And most importantly, head coach Mike Sertich impressed me. I had a funny feeling he was just the kind of coach I needed.

But I wanted to make one thing perfectly clear before I accepted Sertich's offer of a full scholarship.

"When I come to Duluth," I said. "I'm coming as Brett Hull, not Bobby Hull's son."

"We recruited Brett Hull," Sertich said. "We think he's a much better player than Bobby Hull's son."

We shook hands on the deal.

ST. LOUIS

CHAPTER 4

BULLDOGS
AND
BEARS

Once you have been chased by a bear, a growling NHL defenseman doesn't seem quite so menacing.

Minnesota-Duluth teammate Jim "Tonto" Toninato and I were looking for a gas station on the outskirts of Duluth, when our car choked dead on its last ounce of fuel. We had just started walking, when we spotted a 250-pound black bear moseying out of the woods about thirty yards up the road.

This wasn't Yogi, or Boo Boo. We started laughing nervously.

"Well, Tonto, what are we supposed to do?"

"I have no idea."

"What do you mean, you have no idea? I'm from Vancouver. I don't know bears. You're from Bemidji, Minnesota. You know bears."

"Well, I don't know this bear."

My bright idea was to tip-toe up the road and hope the bear didn't see us. The bear's idea was to send us on a butt-hauling sprint in the other direction. A 250-pound bear can be inspirational. As soon as he turned toward us, I transformed into Rocket Ismail. At the fifty-yard mark, I was pushing Mach 1. It's the only time I've dedicated that much energy to running without a coach chewing on me.

It was like that old joke: "Brett, why are we running? We can't outrun a bear."

"It's not the bear I'm trying to outrun," I said, trying to inch ahead of Tonto.

We don't know whether the bear actually took more than a few steps toward us, because neither of us had the courage to turn around. I found out later that black bear attacks usually involve a mother protecting her cubs. We didn't feel that we had time to determine the bear's sex and ask to see a family album. When we were too exhausted to run farther, we both collapsed into hysterical laughter.

Welcome to Duluth, Minnesota, population 85,000; not the place of my birth, but somewhere I can call home.

I liked Duluth the first time I visited, in the spring of 1984. Coach Mike Sertich calls it "the best-kept secret in North America." It has a big city's hustle, without losing the charm and ease of small-town life. Lake Superior, a mile or so from central campus, provides the city's postcard views. No matter where you are in Duluth, you are never more than thirty minutes away from an inland lake. Nor are you that far from woods so dense that even a 250-pound black bear could get lost. Even the climate is a lure: you freeze all that is dear to you in the winter. But the payback is the most pleasant summer climate known to man. The nation could be drenched in sweat from a coast-to-coast heat wave, and Duluth would be 75 degrees with a cool breeze blowing off nearby Lake Superior.

The Bulldogs fans are great. When Dad came to see me play against Harvard, he said the Duluth fans reminded him of fans at Chicago Stadium. "These Duluth fans whip players into such a crescendo, they want to fly." Hockey is the only Division I sport at Minnesota-Duluth; it's the biggest show in town.

Duluth is a place that either draws you back, or keeps you from leaving. Eight or nine of my Minnesota-Duluth teammates live there or go there for the summer. I bought a house there, on Pike Lake, last season. Edmonton Oilers defenseman Norm Maciver is a summer resident. Former Chicago Blackhawks player Bill Watson, who scored forty-nine goals during my freshman year at UMD, is coaching at St. Scholastica College. His linemates, Tom Herzig and Matt Christensen, both settled in the city. Herzig is a dentist.

My girlfriend, Alison, is also from Duluth. Her dad owned the Warehouse Bar, which was the official Monday hangout of the UMD players. I met her during my freshman year, and we have been together ever since.

Duluth is also the place where I learned to take my game to a higher level. Sertich was the coach I needed at that point in my career. He stressed skating, using a program first adopted by the gold-medal-winning 1980 U.S. Olympic team. Every Monday and Wednesday, we practiced without pucks. I hated it. But I needed it. For forty-five to fifty minutes, he skated us like a drill sergeant taking recruits through basic training.

The summer before arriving at UMD, I had gotten all bruised up in a dirt bike accident. When I arrived, I was out of shape. Maciver still jokes with me about being stunned when he saw me practice for the first time.

"They kept talking about how we were going to get this big scorer," Maciver said, "and I looked at you and wondered if you would even be able to make the team."

My first dose of Sertich's dryland training turned out to be eventful. We showed up, then Sertich and assistant coach Glenn Kulyk said we were all going "out for a little run."

His little run was six miles. All but two of the guys were finished after forty-five minutes. At that point, my new teammate Dave Cowan and I were still ten minutes out. We decided to take a shortcut through a parking lot, which would have cut some considerable distance off our run. Really, it was my idea. We were so out of breath that we almost ran into a guy walking through that parking lot.

"Sorry ... Oh, Coach Kulyk ... Geez, we must have taken a wrong turn."

This may sound surprising, but I went to UMD because Sertich's practices were tough. When Sertich recruited me, I told him I wanted to improve on my skating and defense. He promised me I would. His word was good. He pushed me hard. He pushed everyone hard.

"If you quit on me now, you'll quit on me in the third period," he would say, when his skating drills had us all gasping.

Not even stars were immune from prosecution. Bill Watson won the Hobey Baker that season, with Sertich hounding him at every practice. But at least Sertich wrapped his criticism in humor.

"Hull and Watson," he would say, "you're getting slower every day, and today you're skating like tomorrow."

Every time Watson and I skated together in drills, he would pick on us for our lack of speed.

"It's bad enough that you guys skate like you're carrying a piano on your back," Sertich would say. "But do you have to stop and play it too?"

The key to surviving Sertich's drills was finding the right dance partners. We divided ourselves into lines, and my objective was avoiding players who made me look slower than I was.

Okay, let's size up our options. I could go with Herzig and [soon-to-be NHLer] Jim Johnson in one line. No, they're way too fast.

How about Christensen's line? No, he works too hard.

Well, what about Skeeter Moore, Bruce Fishback and Joe Delisle? Nah, they're too eager to look good, because they're trying to stay in the lineup.

There's Cowan, Watson and Maciver. Oh yeah, those guys are just right. None of those guys are ever going to be mistaken for Paul Coffey.

"Hey, Billy, they can call us the piano line," I joked, joining the group that Sertich referred to as "The Hiders."

We called Coach Sertie or Serts. If we lost on Saturday or Sunday, he could be a black bear to live with on Monday. Still, he was a fair coach who knew when to let the horses run.

What I liked about Sertich was that he didn't try to change the way I played the game. "If you are a thoroughbred," he told me when he recruited me, "I won't try to make you into a plow horse."

Sertie believed a team's playing style should be dictated by its personnel.

"The Boston Celtics are a good example of that," he said. "Larry Bird wasn't a typical Celtics player. But when they got him, they changed their style to take advantage of his talent. I think a coach has to look at what he has, before he decides what he's going to do."

Sertie used to say that hockey games come down to two-on-one breaks. "If you always score on your two-on-ones, and prevent the other team from getting two-on-ones, you'll probably win."

He also believes that, once the game begins, it is players — not coaches — determining the outcome.

"Any coach who believes he's deciding the game is fooling himself," Sertie said.

All that he asked was that I improve each game. In that respect, he was very similar to St. Louis Blues coach Brian Sutter.

Sertie was also ready with a one-liner or slogan for all occasions. He's had one message inscribed on a paperweight that has sat on his desk for ten years. It greets any player who comes to the office to see him: "It isn't the mountains ahead that wear you out, it's the grains of sand in your shoes."

My career might have been altered considerably, had Sertie been the kind of man who was tempted by money, ego, or both. After my freshman year, he was offered a higher-profile coaching job at the University of Minnesota. More prestige. A salary increase of $12,500. Sertie turned it down. Duluth is a difficult place to leave.

In that first year, Sertie literally skated my cheeks off. I didn't realize how much better-conditioned I was, until I returned to Vancouver at the end of the school year.

"Brett, you look great," brother Bart said, with an impish grin. "This is the first time I ever knew you had cheekbones."

College hockey took its time adjusting to my game. Playing on the second line with Danny May and Mark Odnokon, I had only seven goals by Christmas. Three had come in one game against Northeastern on December 14. In eight Western Collegiate Hockey Association games, I had one goal.

The college game was much faster, and I knew it was taking me time to adjust. I actually wasn't worried. But I'm sure people were looking at me wondering what form of inferior competition had allowed this Hull kid to score 105 goals the season before.

But even when I had no goals, I was scoring with teammates. I was accepted instantly. That was important, because I'm sure, at the start of the season, they were probably wondering whether I was going to be a cocky son of a legend. What my new teammates found was that Hullie liked to have a good time on and off the ice. You can be serious about the game without being a saint.

One evening, my new linemate, "Cow" Cowan, not known as a wild night-lifer, announced loudly that he could keep up with his teammates for a night of revelry. Monday night was always the team's night to take control of the Warehouse. Cow decided, one Monday, that he wanted to run with the big dogs.

Watson tried to counsel Cow against such an attempt. "Even though you're a sophomore, and Hullie is a freshman, don't think you can keep up with us," Watson warned. "Trust me, you can't."

Cow valiantly took the bull by horns that night at the Warehouse. But Cow wasn't drinking milk, and the next morning Cow felt like a dog.

The team photo was scheduled for the morning, and Cow was barely among the living when he arrived. He couldn't answer the bell for the afternoon skate.

"I think Cow's got the practice flu," Watson told Sertich.

Everybody cracked up.

If you look at the team picture from 1984-85 you will see a sea of white faces. Of course one of us is smiling. One of us is always smiling.

At Christmas, our team went to the Soviet Union to play two exhibition games against the Soviet junior team and a Soviet college team. We were supposedly the first college team to be invited to play in the Soviet Union, but most of the players didn't want to go. It meant we wouldn't be able to go home for Christmas break.

In Moscow, there was very little to do. One night, we were playing cards in Watson's room. It was very late when Tonto and I headed back to our room. I can't remember why or how we started to play-fight. The next thing we knew, we were rolling around in the hallway and slamming up against someone's door.

Now, there were probably two hundred doors on that floor, but we happened to hit this certain one with a bang. Of course, a man sleepily answered the door. We instantly recognized him as Bruce McLeod, our school's athletic director.

There wasn't much left to say at that point, except, "Good morning, Mr. McLeod."

In early December, Sertich moved me to the third line with Cowan and Moore. We clicked immediately. At one point, I had a twelve-game scoring streak, and finished with twenty-five goals in my final twenty-eight games. My thirty-two goals for the season broke Bill Oleksuk's school record for goals by a freshman. I was named Western Collegiate Hockey Association freshman of the year.

Sertie told the local newspaper I was a good example of what hard work can do. More so, I was an example of how Sertich helps players reach their peak performance. I learned more in my first season in Duluth than I learned in all the previous years I had played hockey.

I'm basically a lazy person, and Sertich showed me how to work, and what benefits can be gained by work. I had four goals in my first eighteen games and twenty in my next sixteen. Clearly, I didn't anticipate how much faster college hockey would be. For a short period, I even wondered if I was out of my league. I was tenative, hanging back, not being anything like the Brett Hull who considers the opposition zone his second home.

The new line helped me rediscover my game. Cow was the playmaker, and Skeeter was the haymaker.

Skeeter was a gritty guy, about 5-foot-7, 165 pounds, who always seemed to be in the middle of every scrap.

"You must have driven your mom crazy," Sertich said to Skeeter. "When you were a kid, I'll bet you crossed the street first and then looked to see if cars were coming."

With three lines playing well, the team was on a roll. From January 26 through March 8, we won eleven in a row. We were the Number One team in the nation. Included in that span was my best weekend as a collegiate player. I had back-to-back hat tricks against Wisconsin. The Badgers turned out to be my favorite opponent. In eight games against Wisconsin, I had thirteen goals over two seasons.

I had another hat trick the following season against Wisconsin goaltender Mike Richter. Everyone talks about one shot that went whizzing by Richter's head without him moving. But I really don't remember that happening. I do remember Sertie telling me to test Richter, because he was a freshman goaltender.

"Grease him with a high one a couple of times, and let's see how he reacts," Sertie said.

I never really did that, because I don't fire for show. I fire for effect. My attitude about goaltenders is simple: all of them are good, or they wouldn't be there.

I do know goaltenders don't care for my shots, when they sail high. During my freshman year, UMD had an excellent goaltender named Rick Kosti. He posted a 33-9-3 record that season with a 3.20 goals-against average, while earning All-American status.

But he wasn't fond of facing my shots during practice — mostly because I was careless. As my shots rose to eye-level, he vacated the net. There were times when he would see it was my turn to shoot, and he would just skate out of the net.

Reserve Ben Duffey, who played only twenty-eight minutes all season, would have to replace him in goal. Poor Duff was almost our target-practice goaltender. Once, Watson hit him on the left side of the helmet with a wicked riser. Then I came down the next time and hit the right side of his helmet with a hard blast. When he pulled his mask off, he had the same look the coyote has after the roadrunner has dropped a second boulder on his head.

No one blamed Kosti for not putting up with my careless shooting. He knew I would send them high, not to hurt him, but to get a rise out of him. He was a proven college goaltender and didn't need that nonsense. Since then, I'm a lot more responsible with my shots.

The only time I ever hurt anyone seriously with my shot was during a freak accident at a Duluth practice. During a five-on-five drill, I was off balance when I one-timed a shot that caught defenseman Mike DeAngelis at the place where the face-mask ends and the flesh begins. He needed two hours of surgery to repair a broken jaw.

DeAngelis, who played with me at Penticton, knew it was just an accident.

"If I hadn't flinched and turned my head, it would have hit me right on the helmet," he said.

Our post-season success started with a 6-2 victory against Minnesota, to win the WCHA playoff championship.

Then, we defeated Harvard 4-3 and 4-2 at a NCAA quarterfinal matchup, to earn a berth in the semifinal against Rensselaer Polytechnic Institute, at Detroit's Joe Louis Arena. This was especially sweet because many of the guys had been around the year before, when UMD lost to Bowling Green during the fourth overtime of the NCAA championship game, in Lake Placid. They wanted another shot at the final.

Beating RPI wasn't going to be easy. The team came into the game with a thirty-three-game unbeaten streak. The Engineers goaltender was Daren Puppa, now the Number One netminder for the Buffalo Sabres.

We kept falling behind. We were down 3-2, and I beat Puppa on a breakaway to tie the score, with thirty-six seconds left in the second period. Defenseman Brian Johnson fed me the pass from just inside our blue line. He hit me in stride at the RPI blue line.

My shot hit Puppa's pad and bounced into the net. The Engineers then went ahead again, before Watson scored at 7:04 of the third period, to tie the score, 4-4. Then Herzig scored on a thirty-foot wrist, to put us ahead 5-4 with 6:50 left in the game. Veterans remembered the year before, when the Bulldogs gave up a late tying goal to Bowling Green in regulation, then lost the heartbreaker in the longest final in NCAA history.

We were all concentrating on defense — maybe too much. There was a scramble behind our goal, and the puck was centre to Ken Hammond, who tapped it in from four feet for the tying goal, with 1:57 left. We were going to OT. It was *deja vu* for many of our players.

Sertie warned us between periods that, if we kept thinking about the tying goal, we would probably surrender the winning goal in a hurry.

We played well; the tie remained through two full overtime periods. My linemates, Skeeter and Cow, had the best scoring chance in overtime for us; Skeeter made a great play, to bring the puck around the net on a wrap-around play. And Cowan just missed banging in the centring feed.

At the end of the second overtime, our team was involved in one of the costliest scuffles in school history. It also had to be the strangest call in NCAA history. All I can tell you is that RPI's Pierre Langevin ran Mark Baron hard into the boards, as the period ended. Immediately, there was pushing and jabbing with sticks, among the players on the ice. Watson, who watched the incident from the bench, somehow was penalized two minutes for roughing. To this day, no one has ever figured out how or why Watson was penalized. Sertie still believes RPI coach Mike Addesa convinced the officials that Watson was on the ice.

Baron, who had scored two goals for us earlier in the game, ended up with six minutes in penalties. RPI penalties included four minutes to Ken Hammond and two to Langevin.

The most amazing aspect of Baron's penalty was that he was among the least-penalized players on the team. In thirty-four league games, he had just five minor penalties.

"This game is starting to remind me way too much of Bowling Green," Maciver said, with the appropriate amount of bitterness.

The net result of the incident was a RPI power-play in the third overtime. We played three-on-three for the first two minutes of the third overtime. Then we played four-on-four for two minutes, before we were faced with trying to kill a two-minute power play. At 5:45 of the third overtime, John Carter scored the game-winner for RPI, on a forty-five-foot slap shot that hit Johnson's stick in front of the net. The Engineers went on to beat Providence for the national championship.

One more thing I need to tell you about the game against RPI. I rarely notice anyone I'm playing against. There is always too much going on, to keep tabs of the opposition's lineup.

But RPI had one dynamite player. A crafty play-maker, he set a NCAA record with five assists in that game.

His name was Adam Oates.

Bobby, Brett, Blake, Bob Jr. and Joanne Hull, 1965.

Joanne (right) in the Ice Show at the Conrad Hilton Hotel.

Bob Jr., Blake, Brett, Joanne and Bobby Hull at the Chicago
Black Hawks' Christmas party, 1966.

Bob Jr., baby Michelle, Joanne, Blake, Bart,
Bobby and Brett Hull, 1970.

Blake and
Brett Hull
at Brett's
third birth-
day party.

Christmas 1970 with Santa and the
Black Hawks: (back row, from left)
Bobby, Michelle, Joanne, Brett; (front
row, from left) Bob Jr., Blake, Bart.

At home in Chicago: Brett, Bart, Michelle, Joanne,
Bob Jr. and Blake.

At the Winnipeg Jets' Christmas party 1975: (back) Brett, Bob Jr., Blake; (front) Bart, Michelle.

In Winnipeg: (back) Blake, Joanne, Bob; (front) Bart, Michelle, Brett.

Brett and Joanne Hull in North Vancouver circa 1980.

Captain of the Tuxedo Jets, 1973-74.

Brett (back row, second from right) with the North Shore
Winter Club, 1980-81.

ST. LOUIS

CHAPTER 5

PLAYING
A MAN
SHORT

A cop came looking for me during the 1985-86 season, and I wasn't even worried.

It was part of the local newspaper's efforts to determine the speed of one of my slap shots. Duluth police sergeant Patrick Nichols brought his radar gun to Pioneer Hall practice arena, with the hope of obtaining a miles-per-hour reading.

By then, my shot was a source of curiosity both at home and away. I was en route to the rare college feat of a fifty-goal season, and everyone figured the shot was the secret of my success.

Every time we visited a city, there would be story providing a broken-stick tally, plus eyewitness descriptions of what a horror show I supposedly was for opposing goaltenders.

Equipment manager Rick Menz was a popular source for reporters wanting to write about me. He'd tell them all the same tale, about how I broke more sticks than any player in Bulldogs history. He'd tell them I was breaking two or three wooden sticks a day, before switching to an aluminum shaft. Even then, I still broke two blades per day. "At least now," Rick said, "the shaft was good for a week."

Yeah, right. First, there are guys in all leagues who shoot the puck as hard or harder than I do. Secondly, I can tell you there has never been a goaltender who bailed out on one of my shots. OK, maybe one. He was on the Polish National team. I'm not making this up.

During the 1986 World Championships in Moscow, I was playing for Team USA. With two goals already on the scoresheet from decent shots, I was carrying the puck over the blue line.

When I cocked my stick, the Polish goaltender had all but decided to pull the chute. I ripped the shot, as he yanked the ripcord. He was half-way to Warsaw as the puck found the net, to complete my hat trick.

In some arenas, fans would taunt me during warmup — *oohing* and *aahing* at a shot. At the University of Denver, fans roared with delight every time I broke a stick in warmup.

Teammates were more curious than astounded by my shot. They would check out the pattern of my stick's blade and talk to me about the mechanics of shooting a puck.

"All I know," Tonto said to me one day, "is you score from places I wouldn't even dream of shooting from."

"You don't score if you don't shoot," I repeated for the thousandth time.

Kevin Pates, a reporter for the *Duluth News-Tribune & Herald*, wanted to see how close I could get to my dad's 118.3-miles-per-hour shot, which is listed in the *Guinness Book of World Records* as the fastest slap shot.

Dad's slap shot was supposed to have been thirty-five miles per hour faster than the average NHL shot during the 1960s.

In Duluth, the gun was stationed at the blue line, and I fired forty shots. Only eight registered on the gun. The best readout was eighty-six miles per hour. My teammates booed me. "C'mon, Brett, you have to shoot it," someone yelled. Because the gun was stationary, Nichols said it would be more accurate if we added five miles per hour. Still, they booed.

Some of the other guys had shots in my neighborhood. Tonto and Sean Toomey both registered at eighty. My concern has always been not how fast my shots go in the net, but how often. During my sophomore season, my shots were filling the net regularly. Matt Christensen was one of the big reasons for my successs.

When right wing Bill Watson signed with the Chicago Blackhawks in the spring of 1985, I inherited one of the best centres in Minnesota-Duluth history.

Christensen was as productive as any college centre playing during the mid-1980s. He created the equivalent of two fifty-goal right-wing scorers — his passing helped Watson score forty-nine in 1984-85, and I had fifty-two in 1985-86.

Christensen was from the Minnesota iron-range town of Hoyt Lakes, population 2,000. He was a rangy, 6-foot-3 player with a long reach and great instincts. He wasn't fast, but possessed awesome ice awareness. I always thought he shot the puck as well as I did. It was so good that Sertich used to move him back to the point, and put defenseman Maciver at centre sometimes, on the power play. He was like a bigger version of former St. Louis Blues standout Bernie Federko.

Herzig, who was Christensen's left wing in 1984-85, also graduated. So Skeeter Moore moved up to the Number One line with me. The Moore-Christensen-Hull chemistry was good almost immediately — I had sixteen goals during our first nine games, and Matt assisted on almost all of them. I finished with a UMD-record seven hat tricks, and I'm sure he assisted on seventy-five percent of those goals.

UMD won thirteen of its first sixteen games, and we started to believe we had a chance to win an unprecedented third-consecutive WCHA title. We thought we could make another run at a national title.

It was a season of great fun. Sertie was as quick-witted as ever. I was always forgetting a tie, or sport-coat, or something on road trips. He would just shake his head.

"Hullie, you're amazing," he said. "How is that you know exactly where you were on the ice at 18:39 of the third period in a game that happened last week, but you can never remember where you left your sunglasses or wallet?"

Even practices were a good time. One day we were in a shooting drill, and all of my shots ripped into the net.

"First there was the Great Gretzky," Sertich yelled. "Now there is the Great Brettzky."

The guys just hooted. They loved it. Reporters picked it up — it even appeared in a *Sports Illustrated* story — and it stuck for a while. Of course nobody cared that I hated it. Wayne Gretzky is the greatest hockey player ever, and it just isn't right to have a nickname derived from his nickname.

That's the same reason why I have never liked the nickname Golden Brett or the Golden Knight when I was in Penticton. Dad is the Golden Jet, and he is the greatest left wing ever to play. It's just not cool for me to use a derivative of his nickname. If it's all the same, just call me Hullie or Hullsy. That I like.

I may lead the league in nicknames. Over the years, I've had many. As a teen-ager in North Vancouver, I was known as Pup. Kelly Muir's brother, Kim, stuck me with that one. One day I walked into the Muir house, and Kim looked at me and said, "You got big hands. They look like paws on a puppy." The nickname Pup was born. From there came the Playful Pup, Puppy, Pupster, Doggie and Dogger. Another time, my wide girth and gentle demeanor prompted friends to call me Huggy Bear.

My Penticton teammates sized up a build that was round in the middle and normal on top, and decided I should be called Pickle.

When I came to Minnesota-Duluth, Sertich told me I was an NHL-calibre prospect. He said I would probably sign a pro contract before my four years of eligibility were over. I didn't have that kind of confidence level in my first season. In my second year, I found my comfort level.

I was accustomed to all the media attention, and accustomed to being someone the team counted on for big goals. I was even accustomed to being the villain on the road. I remember playing at the University of Lowell and no one was heckling. I missed it.

The Calgary Flames, who owned my NHL draft rights, were starting to pay attention to my success. Flames scout Al Godfrey saw me regularly. I heard the Flames were thinking about signing me after the season. That certainly fit their gameplan. After Wisconsin coach Bob Johnson joined the Flames as coach, in 1982, scouts started to spend more time on college campuses. There were nine former college players on the Flames' roster that season.

My confidence level was strangely similar to the level of my last season in Penticton. That year, I remember getting goals forty-seven through fifty during one game before Christmas.

In my sophomore year at UMD, I remember driving to the rink with Maciver before a playoff game against Northern Michigan. I had forty-six goals, and there was a chance our season would be over if we lost.

"I'm going to get my fiftieth tonight," I boasted.

Maciver laughed. "Whatever you say, Hullie."

We won that game 8-4, and after I scored my fourth goal of the game I skated by Maciver. "I told you so."

In February, we were ranked Number One in the nation, but we were still fighting for first place. February 8 was a big night for us. After losing at home to Wisconsin the night before, we came back the next night to win 5-3 and move within a point of first place in the WCHA.

Christensen had the game-winning goal and assisted on my two goals. He had sixteen goals and forty-one assists in thirty-three games. He needed just three points to tie Dan Lempe's school record of 222 points, set between 1976 and 1980. Matt was pumped. He was a ninth-round draft pick of the St. Louis Blues, and it was pretty clear they were going to sign him after the playoffs. He had decided on an agent. If we could win a national title, his bargaining power might be even greater.

We only had four WCHA games remaining — two at Minnesota and two at Northern Michigan — and we believed we were headed for another good post-season run. Although we had lost our leading scorer and top goaltender from the previous year, we had jelled into a solid team.

None of us could have possibly known, the night we beat Wisconsin, our world was about to be turned inside out. A third consecutive hockey title, which had seemed so important to us, became insignificant.

The team attended a charity bowl-a-thon Sunday, in nearby Hermantown. Most of the guys were looking forward to it. Not me. I had been kneed in the thigh during the game against Wisconsin, and I used that as an excuse not to show up. Bowling just isn't my idea of a good time.

After the bowl-a-thon everyone went to play boot hockey in Duluth Heights, at the home of a hockey booster. Everyone was running around the ice, whacking the tennis ball and having great fun. No one gave much notice when Matt dropped his stick for the first time. But when he wasn't able to pick it up, guys knew something was wrong. Seriously wrong. With his teammates running to him, Matt collapsed.

He was rushed to the hospital, and at first, doctors thought he'd had a seizure. Then, a CAT scan revealed he had had a stroke.

That news devastated everyone. Matt was a quiet guy, never rocked the boat, and was not a big-time party guy. Maciver had bowled next to him all afternoon and never noticed a thing. I freaked when I heard. By the time I got to the hospital, the guys were like zombies. Matt was a twenty-one-year-old in great shape. He had missed just two games in his four-year Minnesota-Duluth career. How can you be scoring a game-winning goal on Saturday night, and on Sunday night be lying in a hospital bed, partially paralyzed? It seemed too unreal, but it was all too true.

Most of us wanted to know why it had happened. And could it happen to us?

We tried to practice Monday, but everyone's attitude was gloomy. It was the quietest practice you've ever seen. No one wanted to be there. The news went from bad to worse Tuesday, when Matt suffered a second stroke. Horribly, this one was even worse than Sunday's.

Matt's parents were amazingly strong during the crisis. Elliott Christensen, a retired Hoyt Lakes police officer, and his wife, Marge, had dealt with family trauma before. In 1972, their oldest son, Tim, had broken nearly every bone in his body during a car accident. Matt's family displayed more courage than the hockey players.

For almost two days, Matt was in a life-threatening situation, as the doctors used anti-coagulant medication to dissolve the clot in an artery near his brain. Serts told us that it looked like it was sixty-forty that he would be OK.

By Thursday, he seemed to be improving. We wore his Number 7 patches on our uniforms, and talked about winning for him. Sertich did all that he could to keep our spirits up, but we were toast. We had lost our will to win, and Sertich knew it.

We lost 4-3 and 6-3 at Minnesota, then the following weekend we lost twice at Northern Michigan. After Matt's stroke, the team was 1-5-2. We ended up in fourth place.

Matt did recover, and if you saw him on the street today in Duluth, where he still lives, you wouldn't suspect what happened. It's really a fantastic story.

His dream of an NHL career never happened, but he has played at some charity games at UMD, and plays some golf. He was one of the guys who helped turn me into a golf addict.

He was allowed to visit us before we entered the playoffs. Sixteen days after the stroke, he was beating on the plexiglass to give us encouragement. We survived Northern Michigan with a win and a tie, but we were eliminated by a loss and a tie at Denver the following week.

Even before Matt's stroke, I was never one to over-dramatize the importance of a hockey game. I play hard, but I don't approach the game as if I'm out there searching for a cure for cancer. I can't be that serious about it. I just try to have fun. And if you're having fun, you're probably playing at your best.

Serts said later, "A teammate's life is in limbo, and we're getting on a bus on Thursday to go play a hockey game. To me it seemed kind of stupid."

ST. LOUIS

CHAPTER 6

FLAME OUT

My first agent might be the only guy in North America who has both a Harvard law degree and a tattoo on his rear end.

When I was thinking about signing with the Calgary Flames in May 1986, it was clear Brian Burke was the best available agent. About a zillion agents called me during my sophomore season at Minnesota-Duluth. Even Dad, who I had only seen a couple of times in seven years, wanted to represent me.

I hadn't planned to join the NHL after my sophomore year. I remember telling reporters in December that I was coming back for my junior year.

"I didn't come all this way to go to school for just two years," I said.

But after Flames General Manager Cliff Fletcher came, on February 16, to watch me play against the University of Minnesota, I began to think seriously about leaving. Fletcher told me the Flames probably would make me an offer. I figured I'd be able to tell whether I could play in the NHL by the size of their offer.

That's when Burkie stepped in. He actually picked me, more than I picked him. That's how he operated. He was choosy about his clients and wouldn't accept anyone until after a lengthy meeting. He interviewed us more than we interviewed him, when he came to meet Mom, Harry and me in Vancouver. He was up-front about NCAA regulations. He said he didn't want my eligibility jeopardized if I didn't turn pro.

I also liked that Burkie's testosterone level was at the flood stage when he negotiated. College players weren't getting one-way contracts in those days, but he assured Harry and Mom that I would.

"The Flames want you," Burkie said. "They'll give you one, or you're staying in Duluth."

Burkie was built like a refrigerator. He was 6-foot-2, 220 pounds, when he played right wing at Providence. His coach was Lou Lamoriello, now the general manager of the New Jersey Devils. Burkie thinks the world of Lamoriello, which is amazing, considering that Lamoriello once punished him by making him skate at four a.m. for nine days. If someone sentenced me to a pre-dawn skate for nine days, I wouldn't be sending him Christmas cards every year.

Burkie's sin was being late for a Christmas-morning practice. He had slept in after taking three freshmen to midnight mass. I'm surprised Lamoriello just didn't have him publicly flogged for such a heinous act.

"But I'll tell you what," Burkie said. "That was the last time I was ever late for anything."

He later played one season for the Calder Champion Maine Mariners of the American Hockey League in 1977-78. He was undefeated in ten fights, but quit the game because he wasn't going anywhere.

"I was a low-scoring, low-skilled player, and those players aren't exactly in demand," he said.

Burkie is also a proud Irishman. He still balks at working on St. Patrick's Day, a holy day of obligation for the Irish. He likes to go to 6:30 a.m. mass that day, then head to an Irish pub and stay all day. While at Providence, he and a few of his buddies — Jimmy Rafferty, Bill Fahey, Danny McDonald and Peter Malloy — all agreed to have shamrocks tattooed on their bodies. Burkie had his put on his hip. Now that's being Irish down to your shorts.

Even Sertich liked Burkie, because he played by the rules and didn't actively recruit. You almost had to come to him — then you had to pass the interview.

He was big on preparing for life after the game. He authored Burke's Rules, governing what clients could do with money from their first contracts.

You could only spend $15,000 on a new car, and he had limits on other purchases. He gave his clients a long sheet of anticipated expenses, and spelled out how much money you needed to live in professional hockey.

Goaltender Rick Kosti, a teammate at Minnesota-Duluth, talked to Burkie about representing him. He told Burkie he was thinking about buying an expensive car and spending a couple of thousand on clothes. Burkie told him he better find someone else.

"He didn't pass the interview," Burkie said.

One thing Burkie and I agreed on was that Sertich was to be kept informed of my decisions every step of the way. I respected Sertich, and I owed him that courtesy.

Let me also say this about leaving college after two years: it's the only regret I've ever had in my life. Playing in Duluth was everything I dreamed about when playing hockey. Great town. Great time. Great hockey. Great people.

As you might expect, Sertich originally was against me turning pro. All he asked was that I remember a college degree is more valuable than a season, or two seasons, of minor-league money.

"I think Canadian kids tend to jump at the NHL a little quicker than Americans," he told me. "Canadians grow up thinking *I'm going to be on Hockey Night in Canada*. Americans think, *I'm going to play college hockey, get a degree, maybe play in the Olympics and maybe turn pro*. I just want you to make sure you only sign for a great deal. Don't go for just a good deal."

Sertich was sure I was thinking right, when we told him we wanted a $150,000 signing bonus and the one-way contract or I would return to Duluth. A one-way contract pays the same amount even if you are playing in a minor league. Most players receive two-way contracts: their NHL salary might be $110,000, but they would probably be paid about $35,000 if they got sent to the minors.

The one-way contract demand was more than a little brassy on our part. Fletcher had signed several talented college free agents — including Joel Otto, Jamie Macoun, Ed Beers, Gino Cavallini and Neil Sheehy — without giving any of them a one-way contract. But Burkie believed we were in a great bargaining position. The Flames believed they could win the Stanley Cup that season. They were looking for a goal scorer they could add to the lineup, and my fifty-two goals must have looked rather attractive.

It probably didn't hurt my situation that I had led Team USA in scoring, with seven goals and four assists at the World Championships that spring in Moscow. We knew Calgary Coach Bob Johnson had even flown to Denver to watch me play at the end of the season.

"If the Flames don't give you the one-way," Burkie said, "you'll go back and score seventy-five goals as a junior. Next spring, we'll be asking for more money than we're asking for now."

Under the goofy NCAA rules, Burkie wasn't allowed to negotiate for me, without jeopardizing my eligibility. He could only advise me. So he called Fletcher to say I was willing to listen to offers, and he would be advising me.

"But if it's not a one-way contract," Burkie told him, "I'm going to recommend he not sign it."

Fletcher laughed. "He can stay in school then. We've given two-way contracts to a lot of good college hockey players before Brett."

Burkie said not to worry. "Fletcher is very fair, but he doesn't give money away," he said. "You'll hear from him."

The offer came. It was a two-way contract. I don't even remember for how much. It was rejected. Burkie called Fletcher to tell him my attitude hadn't changed.

"I guess we don't have any options then, because we want to sign him," Fletcher said. "We'll give him the one-way. Let's negotiate."

We agreed on three years, plus an option. The signing bonus was $150,000, and the yearly salaries were $70,000, $105,000, $115,000 and $125,000 — all in U.S. money. It was comical to hear people talking about what a bad contract I had, when I was with the Flames. My first contract actually was a great contract. How many players earn more than $200,000 before making the NHL? I was probably the highest-paid man in Moncton, when I lived there.

You probably want to know what I did with my bonus. Considering my wild teen-age tendencies, you're thinking I probably blew most of it. You're thinking I took a wild trip to the Caribbean. Or bought a Jag, with an elaborate stereo system and 350 cassettes. And you're thinking I took everyone I knew to a David Bowie concert. Wrong.

I put $15,000 in my checking account for living expenses. The car I bought was a '69 Camaro. The remainder went into an annuity, recommended by Harry, that will mature when I'm thirty-two.

When it comes to managing money, I'm as conservative as your neighborhood banker. I tell my investment guys up front, "Don't think you'll get rich buying stocks for Brett Hull."

My conservative business demeanor is the second-greatest Brett Hull legend in my family — distantly trailing my singing voice. When Dad was on the road playing for the Jets, Mom and I occasionally tended the cattle in Winnipeg. I think Mom thought cows stunk as a business venture.

"Whatever you do," she used to tell me, "don't ever invest in anything that eats and poops."

While I was playing in the Canada Cup, Blake tried unsuccessfully to contact me about a business proposition. He finally contacted someone who was going to see me. Blake's first instructions were to tell me that I could make more than $10,000 on the deal.

"Now, the next part you have to write down word for word," Blake told his messenger. "Tell Brett this won't cost him a cent. There is absolutely no risk. If you don't get that part word-for-word, Brett won't call me back."

I'm the Harold Snepsts of investors. Move slowly. Don't take any chances. Accept that you won't score big. Time-deposit certificates. Treasury notes. That's my speed. When I buy CDs, I even go to the side bins. Why pay $14.00, when you can get good music for $7.99?

"Brett," Blake tells me, "you are tighter than a buzzard's butt in a power dive."

Thanks for the compliment. Anyone who thinks I'm working a day after I retire from hockey is sadly mistaken. Being athletic director at Minnesota-Duluth is about the only job that appeals to me as a post-NHL career.

My only misgiving about that first contract was that I only had one option — the Flames. Believe it or not, I really wasn't all that excited about being drafted in June 1984. When the NHL's Central Scouting Service used to send me questionnaires I would send them back unanswered. As a twenty-year-old, it was my last year to be drafted. And someone had told me that I would be better off as a free agent. That was true enough.

Burkie told me that, had I gone undiscovered in Penticton, passed over completely in the draft, I probably would have been asking for a $1.4 to $1.8 million package. That's what Burkie got the Detroit Red Wings to pay Ray Stazsak of Illinois-Chicago that summer when he was a free agent.

The Red Wings were the team that was going after free agents the year I came out. Another guy they signed that year was Adam Oates. He also got a $1 million deal. I have a hunch they would have been interested in me, had I been a free agent.

But money wasn't on my mind when I went to Calgary on May 5, 1986. I was going to a team expected to win the Stanley Cup. Dad had played fifteen seasons, and only won the Stanley Cup in 1960-61. I had a chance to win one in my first four weeks in the NHL. I really believed I could contribute. I figured they wouldn't sign me right after college, if they didn't expect me to play immediately.

Mom, Harry and Bart met me in Calgary. Sertich also came with me. The press conference followed a familiar script.

"How would you compare yourself to your father?"
"I try not to."
"What do you think about your father?"
"I don't think there were many players better than

he was. But I'm my own person, and I hope I don't have to live up to the expectations of his talent."

"Are you excited about following in your father's footsteps?"

"Absolutely. But I didn't see much of him when I was in junior and in college. It's mostly between my mother and step-father that I've come along this far."

I had four years of rehearsal delivering those lines. I had played that part for many reporters in many cities, before I arrived in the NHL.

The Flames put me through a brief workout, and who do you think they put into the goal? I almost died laughing when I looked up and saw it was Rick Kosti, who had been playing for the Flames' Moncton farm team.

He started laughing too. The guy had become absolutely sick of seeing my high shots in practice at Minnesota-Duluth. Now, he turns pro and still has to deal with me.

Calgary Flames scout Glenn Hall, who used to play with my dad, moved from the player's bench to the higher perch in the Saddledome, when I began blasting at Kosti.

"I saw his dad shoot," Hall told reporters. "That's why I'm moving up — to get out of range."

Kosti didn't leave the net once during my shooting drill. "You have to be ready at all times," Kosti told reporters, with a straight face. "He likes to surprise a goaltender. The one thing he improved on when we played together was his accuracy."

The Flames ended up giving me sweater number 16, the number my dad wore when he started with the Blackhawks. (He later switched to number 9). This, of course, was not my first choice. I really wanted number 29, which I had worn in college. But I certainly wasn't to get that from centre Joel Otto. I asked for number 15, but it was already worn by defenseman Robin Bartel. Number 16 was the only good number left.

There is nothing more annoying than a brutal number. Every chance I got, I used to tell former teammate Scott Stevens that he needed a decent number. His number, 2, was a brutal number.

Ironically, the Flames were playing the St. Louis Blues in the Campbell Conference final when I showed up. It was tough series, won by the Flames in seven games.

Boy, it turned out I was wrong to believe they wouldn't sign me unless they wanted to use me. I didn't help my case by showing up out of shape. I had just come from the World Championships in Moscow, where I had led Team USA in scoring, with seven goals and four assists. But there had been too much revelry. I tipped the scales at 211 pounds — ten pounds over my playing weight.

I had no idea what what I was doing. Nor did I know what I faced. But the guys were great. Jim Peplinski, Mike Vernon and Lanny McDonald helped me get acquainted in the dressing room.

Assistant coaches Pierre Page and Bob Murdoch helped me get acquainted with the Flames system, by skating my ass off for an hour after every practice. If you ask me, they took too much delight in that assignment.

The Flames invested considerable time and money to get me on their hockey club, so I could watch from the press box when the Flames beat the Blues 2-1 in Game Seven, to reach the Stanley Cup finals against Montreal. Little did I know the press box would be my second home in Calgary.

We played the first two games at home — winning Game One, 5-3, and losing Game Two, 3-2, in overtime.

But there was some indication I might play in Montreal. After watching the Flames play twenty games in forty-one days, Coach Bob Johnson told the media he thought some players were getting tired. He said he would like to rest about seven players. Steve

Bozak and Hakan Loob hadn't even got a shot on goal in Game Two. Otto was in a goal-scoring slump. And the Flames' injury list was getting longer. Joe Mullen had been out with a bad neck. Patterson was in the hospital with a fever.

Johnson told reporters he was thinking about putting me in the lineup, to spark some goal-scoring. Then came the funny part: "Plus, he weighs 211 pounds. He can play physically if it becomes a physical game."

Who me? This was a future Lady Byng winner he was talking about.

Johnson didn't call me into his office to tell me I was going to play. My first clue was Murdoch and Page not calling me over for the daily torture session. I bet that ruined their day.

You mean you aren't going to skate me until I drop? I was thinking. *I guess that means I'm going to play.*

May 20, 1986. It's Game Three of the Stanley Cup final in the Montreal Forum. Johnson has decided to rest Mike Eaves and Paul Baxter. I'm the new blood in the lineup, along with Yves Courteau, Perry Berezan and Terry Johnson.

I'm in awe. I'm so nervous I can barely lace my skates. How many players in NHL history have started their careers in the Stanley Cup finals? There are probably others, but Edmonton's Kelly Buchberger is the only other I know.

My attendance is required at all Flames' power play meetings, so I know Johnson is planning to use me there if I ever get into a game. Power plays were my playground in college. In my final season at Duluth, I had twenty power-play goals in forty-two games. But I fret all day, because I don't have my own sticks yet. I've been using Mullen's and McDonald's, and neither one feels quite right.

At 2:18 of the first period, Montreal's Craig Ludwig draws a penalty for high sticking. Now I'm on the power-play. My first NHL scoring chance happens immediately. The puck is on my stick, and I fire a wrister that beats Patrick Roy. But it clangs loudly off the post. That post probably still has a mark on it from my shot. I have a few more scoring chances, but only one shot on goal in my debut. We lose, 5-3.

I also played during Game Four in Montreal, when we lost 1-0. I didn't even get a shot on goal. We ended up losing the series in six games. There was a parade back in Calgary, but I didn't stay. Because I joined the team so late, I really didn't feel like I was a Flames player.

I had no idea then that I *never* would feel like a Flames player.

CHAPTER 7

BURNED TO A CRISP

What bothered me about the Calgary Flames was their insistence on reducing hockey to a chin-up competition.

If you could do a million pushups, chin-ups and situps, the Flames' coaches believed you were a good player. If you couldn't, the coaches believed you were a bad player. To that way of thinking, I was a bad player. Very bad.

It never seemed to matter how well I did on the ice. They seemed to care more about physical prowess than offensive production. Even if I scored a goal in every game, I was labled a bad player unless I could win an aerobics contest.

Hey, I'm a hockey player, not a decathlete. Conditioning, obviously, is very important in hockey. Better conditioning has helped me elevate my game. Blues assistant coach Bob Berry rides me about keeping my weight in check, and I sincerely thank him for it. Still, the Blues accept that I can be a major contributor without being Charles Atlas. The Flames could not. My point is that conditioning isn't the only thing that decides hockey games. If it was, the NHL would be scouting for players in YMCA classes.

Wayne Gretzky always finished dead last on the Edmonton Oilers' strength testing, yet it didn't seem to affect his game. Do you think when he came into the league, Glen Sather compared his upper-body strength to Mark Messier and Dave Semenko? I doubt it.

Detroit Tigers first baseman Cecil Fielder, who weighs about 260 pounds on a light day, had an amusing quote about conditioning this summer, when he was in the midst of another home run surge.

"The funny thing is, when I'm hitting home runs nobody asks me how much I weigh," Fielder said. "They only ask me about it when I'm in a slump."

Going into the 1986-87 training camp, there was no question in my mind that I was going to make the Flames' roster. Assistant coach Bob Murdoch called me that summer, to ask about my weight and conditioning. He told me I was "pencilled in" for the following season. He didn't mention that the pencil had an eraser.

A guaranteed spot on the roster made sense to me. Fletcher wouldn't have agreed to a one-way contract — and Johnson wouldn't have used me in the Stanley Cup final — if I wasn't in their plans for the upcoming season. The only potential problem was that right wing was crowded. Incumbents included Lanny McDonald, Mark Hunter, Joe Mullen and Hakan Loob. Still, I figured they might work me in slowly.

"There's always room for a guy who scores," I convinced myself.

Media speculation included a scenario in which Hunter moved to the left wing. Coach Bob Johnson had successfully converted Colin Patterson from the right to left wing. By moving Hunter to left wing, the team could maintain his physical presence while creating a potent right-wing scoring foursome of McDonald, Mullen, Loob and Hull. Each of us had, or would someday, score fifty or more goals during a season.

My offseason preparation included running, but no skating. That may have been a mistake. I was in better shape at the beginning of camp than I had been when I signed the previous May, but the Flames' coaches thought I was a few pounds overweight. Still, I scored four goals and had three assists in the exhibition season. I convinced myself I had made the team.

It looked that way, when the team flew to Boston for the season opener. I had a plane ticket with my name on it. There were rumors around that the Flames were going to trade for Philadelphia Flyers defenseman Brad McCrimmon. There was a chance they could trade a right wing and break up the logjam.

The night before our opener, I went to an American League playoff game between the Boston Red Sox and California Angels, with veterans like Doug Risebrough, Mark Hunter and Paul Baxter. How's that for hanging with the right crowd?

The next morning, I was rocking-and-rolling at the morning skate when Johnson summoned me to the office. He said I was toast. Out of there. Banished to Moncton, to play for some guy with a reputation that read like a Stephen King horror story.

Johnson also demoted left wing Gary Roberts, who was in his third training camp. He told us the Flames couldn't justify carrying seventeen forwards.

He didn't want us sitting in the press box when we could be getting valuable experience in the minor leagues, playing for Terry Crisp.

"I want you to go down there and work on your defense and conditioning, and we'll keep an eye on you," Johnson told me.

I was stunned. I couldn't say anything. I just went back to my hotel room and cried. Then I called Burkie, whose office was in Boston. He met me at the Copley Mariott Hotel.

"It's not the end of the world," he reassured me. "We could have expected this. They're just sending you down for a couple of weeks, while they make some decisions about their personnel. Go down, fill the net, and you'll probably be up in two weeks."

Yeah, that's it. I'm going to be with the Flames and playing regularly in two weeks. But I never could have guessed it would be two seasons later in St. Louis, before I would be considered a full-time NHL player.

I turned into Mr. Diplomacy, talking to reporters about my demotion.

"I'm going down and work hard, so I can be ready when they need me," I said. "I'll get a lot of experience I can use when I get back up there."

I learned a tough lesson in Moncton: how to work for a boss who disliked my approach to both life and hockey. I had a fifty-goal season, and was miserable for most of it. What I learned in almost two seasons with Crisp — one in Moncton and one in Calgary — was that I would never again play in a situation where the game stops being fun. If I ever find myself in another coach-player feud, then I'll either get traded — or I'm quitting. You can't give me enough money to put up with that.

It was nothing against the people in Moncton. They treated me very well. There was only one person in Moncton who gave me a hard time.

The oddity of my relationship with coach Terry Crisp was that I liked him personally. He can very entertaining, very amusing. Reporters love to sit in his office, to get their notebooks filled with lively quotes. He's a great storyteller. He worked hard to earn his place in the NHL, and playing eleven years in the league had provided him with plenty of material. As a player, Crisp wasn't blessed with exceptional talent. Guile and hard work allowed him to score 67 goals in 537 games, during eleven seasons with Boston, St. Louis, the New York Islanders and the Philadelphia Flyers. He earned two Stanley Cup championship rings playing for the Flyers — an accomplishment I can respect.

But I don't think those credentials automatically make you the world's foremost authority on hockey. Crisp thought the only way to play hockey was the way he played it. He thought the way I played the game was wrong. The collision of our philosophies was akin to the jar of Messier and Cam Neely slamming into each other in full stride.

The first three months were the worst. During my first twenty-nine games, I struggled. I thought I was going to be with the Flames, and touring the NHL. Instead, I was off in Moncton with Crisp. I scored just eight goals. Crisp rode me like he was trying to break a wild stallion. He wanted to break my spirit. He wanted to change my life and playing style, simply because he didn't like them.

Crisp often weighed my value as a hockey player by the numbers on the scale at weigh-ins. If I had put on a couple of pounds, he considered it furher evidence I didn't care about hockey.

He tried to remove every ounce of creativity from the game. Every team works on breakouts, but Crisp wanted to map out how to finish three-on-two and two-on-one breaks. He would have it worked out: pass it to the centre. Back to the wing. Over to the far side. It was ridiculous. Once you get into that type of goal-scoring situation, the game becomes improvisational. I like to make it up as I go along. There are far too many variables to follow any script. The goal-tender has no idea what you are going to do, because you have no idea what you are going to do until you do it. I really wasn't interested in Crisp's ideas about goal scoring.

In October, Crisp and I held the summit in his office that was symbolic of our problems for the better part of two seasons. It was the day after he had demoted me to the fourth line for a period. He told me he had called Cliff Fletcher. The dreaded call to Fletcher was one of his favorite threats — and not just to me. So I wasn't devastated by that news. He wanted players to believe he held their livelihood in his hands. He thought fear was a masterful coaching technique.

"You're not working hard enough. I don't like your attitude. You aren't serious enough about making it the NHL," he repeated.

"I don't think you understand me at all," I responded.

So I told him about me. I explained I like the game so much I consider it fun while I'm on the ice. My smile, I said, is not a sign of complacency. It's a response to my love for the game. Enjoying your work doesn't mean you aren't serious about it. I promised him I would watch my weight.

It was obvious my testimony wasn't persuading Judge Crisp, and nothing was resolved. He still wanted to hang me. In hindsight, what he was asking me to do was change my personality. Sure, I was going to change in twenty-four hours what I had developed in twenty-two years. No problem.

I promised to be more demure, to look serious when I was at practice. That was the first and last time I ever promised to be something I am not.

In Moncton, I paid $500 to buy a beat up, four-wheel-drive truck. Roberts and I would cruise around, talking about our predicament.

"It's a joke," I would repeat to Roberts about every ten minutes.

Crisp's power-trip coaching techniques destroyed some guys. Gary would get benched, and his confidence would plummet. When I got benched, I just got mad. "This guy has no clue what he's doing," I would tell Gary.

Confidence is one of the reasons I can score goals. When I was in Moncton, I told myself I was good enough to play for at least eighteen or nineteen of the NHL's twenty-one teams. I just happened to be stuck in an organization with the deepest supply of right wings in world history. I also had this feeling that my NHL performance would be superior to my play in the American Hockey League.

Rumors floated around in early November that Crisp might get the vacant coaching job in Boston. I wasn't the only one hoping he would get it. But my bad luck continued, when the wrong Terry got the Boston job. O'Reilly, not Crisp, was named Boston coach. There were also rumblings that Crisp was going to be hired by the Pittsburgh Penguins. No such luck.

Even though I was brutal for the first eleven games in Moncton, I got called up by Johnson in November. Roberts also got the call. The Flames were running out of bodies. McDonald, Risebrough, Perry Berezan and Brian Bradley all were among the injured.

Harry and Mom came to Calgary to see my first game, on November 14, against Hartford. As soon as Harry realized I had arrived without bringing a coat, he insisted on giving me his. That season, Harry came to see me play three times, and each time he found me without a coat. Each time he gave me his. Goals were difficult to come by in my first few games, but I scored a hat trick in overcoats.

Calgary Herald sportswriter Eric Duhatschek wrote, on November 15, that I had been called up despite the fact that Crisp's reports on me had been "something less than enthusiastic."

"One of the oddities in the Flames organization," Duhatschek insightfully wrote, "is that the major league coach, Johnson, loves college players, but the minor league coach, Crisp, does not."

Johnson put me on a line with Joe Nieuwendyk and Roberts in my first game. It was late in the game, and Gary sent me a rink-wide pass about seven feet in the air. I almost had to jump to catch it. I dropped the puck in front of me, and I cleared the blue line on a breakaway. I blasted it by Steve Weeks. It turned out to be the game-winner. I was thinking, *I'm an NHL player forever.*

"No more godforsaken Moncton," I told Roberts, after the game.

Three games later, I was toast. Back to Moncton. Back to misery. Back to Crisp.

Although I was still miserable, the second half of the season went much better. Brian Bradley was demoted, and he was my centre. In my final thirty-eight games, I scored forty-two goals. I set an AHL record by scoring at least one goal in fourteen consecutive games.

One oddity of my fifty-goal goal season was that my last goal was scored into an empty net on the final weekend of the season — the only empty-net goal I have scored as a professional player.

We were playing the Nova Scotia Oilers; their goaltender was Darryl Reaugh. I had played against him in the BCJHL, four years before. The Oilers and Reaugh shut me down until the third period, when I scored at 7:54 to give Moncton a 5-4 lead. Soon after, I began pressing for the fiftieth.

With 1:45 remaining, I snapped a shot past Reaugh, only to have it clang off the post. Less than a minute later, Nova Scotia Coach Larry Kish did what was expected and pulled his goaltender, so his team could push for the final goal.

Crisp put me on the ice, and I drilled the empty-netter with twenty-eight seconds left.

That may seem like the end of the story, but it wasn't. Two days later, *Moncton Times-Transcript* reporter Dwayne Tingley wrote a column saying Edmonton Oilers General Manager Glen Sather wanted the Edmonton-Calgary rivalry to extend to the minor leagues.

According to Tingley's story, Glen Sather was unhappy with Kish, for giving a Calgary minor-league prospect a chance to score his fiftieth goal into an empty net.

The story quoted an anonymous Oilers source as saying, "We don't give Calgary anything."

My fourteen-game goal streak started on January 16, when Flames Assistant General Manager Al MacNeil came to watch me play against the Nova Scotia Oilers. I had two goals and two assists. Maybe, I figured, I was going to be called up.

The call didn't come until the NHL playoffs. Johnson called me up, played me in four games, and I had two goals and an assist against Winnipeg. After we were eliminated, my reward was being sent back to Moncton for the AHL playoffs.

In retrospect, my year in Moncton had some benefits. At least I can tell younger players that playing in the minor leagues is not the end of the world. "After two or three months in the minors, you will be ten times better as a hockey player," I tell younger players.

If I had never spent a minute in the minors, they would think, *What do you know about it? You've had a cake career. It's all been handed to you.*

But they know now that success hasn't been handed to me. I do know what it's like to be a minor-league slug — to be in the last place you want to be. I do know you can adapt to the situation. And I do know it's possible to overcome anything, or anyone, to get to the NHL.

Johnson quit at the end of the 1986-87 season, to become director of the U.S. amateur hockey program.

Crisp was named head coach. Great. My nightmare had a sequel. Crisp now would be in control of my NHL fate. I sweated, I fretted. Then I tried to be rational: *I scored fifty goals for him last season. Players are supposed to struggle and learn the game in the minors, and I scored fifty goals. He couldn't possibly send me back to the minors.*

Could he?

He didn't demote me the next fall — but he thought about it. The day before the 1987-88 season began, Calgary newspapers discussed whether I might be going to Salt Lake City, Utah, the new home of the Flames' minor league affiliate.

The speculation was that I was going to be the team's fifteenth forward. Crisp pointed out that Loob, Mullen, McDonald and Tim Hunter were still standing in my way. "We don't want him sitting in the press box," Crisp said. "That won't do him any good."

My comment to the newspapers: "If you ask me, sending me back to the minors would set me backwards a million years."

Crisp must have loved that. In Game One, I was in the press box. That was the beginning of the most up-and-down season I had ever known. From day to day, I never had any idea if I would be playing.

The most absurd situation occurred December 3, when I was named NHL Rookie of the Month for November. That night, I was benched for the third consecutive game. During twelve games in November, I scored eight goals with six assists. Nieuwendyk and I were tied for the NHL rookie scoring lead with twenty-three points. He had played four more games than me.

In one stretch between late October and the middle of November, I had ten goals in sixteen games, playing on the line with Mike Bullard and John Tonelli. Bullard and Tonelli were playing great. Tonelli was playing the way he plays best — controlling the corners.

In one game against Montreal, Tonelli hounded Brian Skrudland mercilessly until he finally surrendered the puck. Tonelli perfectly centred the puck on my tape in the slot. I buried it stick-side for the game winner.

On November 15, I scored three goals in the third period — my first NHL hat trick — in an 8-4 win against the Vancouver Canucks. On my final goal, I stole the puck from Randy Boyd and scored on a breakaway.

Eleven days later, Crisp told me he was benching me because he didn't like my overall effort. In particular, he didn't think I was playing well enough defensively.

"Hull is going in circles, rather than straight lines," Crisp told the newspapers.

Funny, I thought I was going straight for the net. You don't get eight goals in twelve games unless you are doing something right.

There was a story in the newspaper, by *Calgary Sun* sportswriter George Johnson, quoting Crisp as saying fans at the Molson Cup Three-Star Luncheon wanted to know when I was going to play again.

Johnson had asked me what I thought Crisp's rationale was for benching me. "I have no idea what he is thinking," I said, honestly. "I have absoutely no idea."

Crisp's reply: "When Lanny sat out, he worked hard and didn't say a word."

Oh, now I'm supposed to surrender, not only my place in the lineup, but my freedom of speech.

Give Crisp credit for courage. He wasn't afraid to risk the wrath of fans. Lanny was one of the most popular players in the city's history, and Crisp benched him without hesitation.

Crisp referred to those he benched as "my buzzards up there [in the press box], waiting for somebody to go bad."

After that exile, I had a two-goal game. I was on parole for fifteen days, then it was back to the press box for a game, then in for three weeks, then out for one, in for one, out for one, then in for two. The situation continued until March 7, 1988, which ranks as the most important date in my professional career.

The day didn't start out that way. Teammate Paul Reinhart and I were headed to the rink for practice. We talked about rumors that circled the team like those buzzards Crisp talked about.

"What do you think is really going on?" I asked, figuring the veteran would know.

"Oh, there's going to be a trade," Rhino assured me. "But I've been around too long, so I'm not going anywhere. You are an up-and-coming goal scorer. Cliff Fletcher doesn't trade top young prospects like you."

"Yeah, but what about the rumors?" I questioned.

"Trust me, Brett," he predicted. "You aren't going anywhere."

ST. LOUIS

CHAPTER 8

MEET ME IN ST. LOUIS

When Terry Crisp told me I had been traded, I couldn't stop smiling. I had to put my head down, because the grin wouldn't go away.

"I just hope it's someplace nice," I said.

"You're going to St. Louis," he said, matter-of-factly.

"*Yesssssss*," I whooped.

It was like an inmate with a life sentence getting an unconditional parole. I was going back to the United States, to play in a nice city for a team that was probably going to play me regularly.

The deal, on March 7, 1988, went like this: the Flames received goaltender Rick Wamsley and defenseman Rob Ramage for Steve Bozek and yours truly. *Calgary Sun* cartoonist Dave Elston had the amusing depiction of St. Louis General Manager Ron Caron, stripped to his underwear, saying to Cliff Fletcher, "Is there anything else I can get you?"

Calgary Herald sportswriter Eric Duhatschek wrote, the following day, "The Calgary Flames added to their murderer's row lineup — but the cost was high."

The cost was high? The cost was high only because I had been a hundred feet off the ice in the press box for the last three games before the trade. I had sat out sixteen of the team's sixty-eight games, when I was traded.

I never asked to be traded. Everyone told me that Fletcher wouldn't trade young prospects. I had no idea St. Louis was interested in me, except that Blues Director of Scouting Ted Hampson had seen me a lot when I played for Penticton. Had the Blues drafted me, both St. Louis and I could have been spared some misery.

It's fair to say I was getting frustrated, playing for Crispy in Calgary. I had spent so much time in the press box, I was starting to use it as my permanent mailing address. If I had spent any more time in Calgary, I might have been become one of the most talented scratches in league history. They could have made a bronze replica of my butt in a chair, and sent it to the Hall of Fame.

My career was a yo-yo. One week I was thrilled, because I was scoring goals regularly and John Tonelli was comparing me to a young Mike Bossy. The next week I was bummed, because Crisp had banished me again to Calgary's buzzard perch.

I was up in the press box thinking, *OK, last week Crisp thinks I'm an NHL player. Now he thinks I can't play.* You don't get confidence, being pulled off the power play. You don't get confidence watching other people play. Every time I was up there, I would worry that, by the time I got back on the ice, I would have lost my scoring touch.

It was difficult to explain to folks outside of Calgary why I wasn't playing. On one hand, I was a Rookie of the Year candidate. I finished with twenty-six goals in fifty-two games with Calgary that season. On the other hand, according to Crisp, I wasn't worth playing on a regular basis. Some were looking for sinister reasons for me being out of the lineup.

A buddy from Vancouver told me there were rumors floating around my hometown that veterans were plotting against me. Fearing I was going to take their jobs, they were taking me out on the town and loading me up with food and booze so I would gain a few pounds and Crispy would stay mad at me. What a joke. That was one of the most ridiculous stories I've ever heard.

Thankfully, the Blues' Caron sorted through the personality conflict with Crisp, to see my true skills as a player. Later, I discovered Caron had first suggested the deal during a chance November meeting with Fletcher at the Dorval Hilton in Montreal. Caron and Fletcher have a friendship dating to their days together as talent hounds for the Montreal Canadiens.

The conversation, according to Caron, went something like this.

Caron: "A goaltender might be all you need to win the Stanley Cup, and I can give you Rick Wamsley. Would you trade Brett Hull?"

Fletcher: "I might, but it's premature to discuss it at this point."

There wasn't really a pressing need for the Flames to make a trade. We were well on our way to finishing first overall. Clearly, we were a top Stanley Cup contender. But Crisp didn't have much faith in Doug Dadswell, who was our backup to goaltender Mike Vernon. And Crisp always wanted a tougher defenseman, someone with a physical presence around the net, someone with criminal intentions.

The Flames had long respected Wamsley. When I signed with Calgary, in May of 1986, the Flames were playing the Blues in the Campbell Conference Final. I didn't play in that series, but I remember Wamsley played well and beat them, 3-2, in Game One at Calgary. He also was in goal in Game Six, when the Blues rallied from a three-goal, third-period deficit to beat the Flames, 6-5, on Doug Wickenheiser's overtime goal. The Flames beat Wamsley, 2-1, in Game Seven. While playing for the Blues, Wamsley was 8-4-0 against the Flames in regular season games.

Two weeks before the trade deadline, Caron called again. At the time, I wasn't even playing regularly; I had sat out four or five games in a row. It didn't appear they wanted me for their post-season run, but Fletcher wasn't about to give me away.

"I'll need a defenseman, too," he told Caron.

That's when Caron brought up Ramage's name.

"It seemed like there was a spark," Caron said later. "There was some interest. So I started to talk, and I can talk until someone tells me to shut up."

Fletcher finally decided to send Assistant General Manager Al MacNeil to scout the Blues game on the Saturday before the trade, and Caron prepared for that game as though it was sting operation. To eliminate the possibility of Wamsley having a poor game, Caron told coach Jacques Martin he wanted him to play Greg Millen. Instead of the truth, he told Martin he wanted to showcase Millen for a possible trade. "Just some reverse psychology," Caron called it later.

He also asked Martin to play Ramage only in favorable situations, like the power play. So basically my whole career hinged on Rob Ramage's ability to impress MacNeil in a few odd shifts on a Saturday night. Of course, I knew none of this, because I was in Calgary trying to figure out how I could score goals from the press box.

Ramage played well in that Saturday game, or at least well enough, because MacNeil called Fletcher immediately after the game from Caron's office. He told Caron, after the call, "I am backing the trade."

Duhatscheck reported later that Fletcher called a meeting of his coaching staff and scouts before the trade.

"Are we prepared to do this trade, knowing Brett Hull may score 160 goals in the next four seasons?" Fletcher asked.

Unanimous.

"Are we prepared to do this trade, knowing Brett Hull may score 180 goals in the next four seasons?"

Unanimous.

"Are we prepared to do this trade, knowing Brett Hull may score 200 goals in the next four seasons?"

Unanimous.

Quebec Nordiques General Manager Pierre Page, who was an assistant coach with the Flames then, still says it was the most difficult trade decision he has ever faced. "We all knew we might get burned," he says.

Immediately after the trade, Fletcher predicted I would score 180 goals over the next four years. He even told me that trading me was breaking his personal rule of never trading a top young prospect.

"We are well aware of what we are doing," Fletcher said. "It's like the commercial on TV. Pay me now or pay me later. Obviously, on this one, we are going to pay later."

What I find amusing is this: if everyone believed I was such an awesome, gifted goal-scorer, why didn't I ever play?. The only ice I saw consistently was in the bottom of my Diet Coke glass. Those nice Fletcher quotes seemed like a real crafty way of covering yourself, in case things went bad.

Fletcher was wrong on his prediction. I didn't get 180 goals in four years. I scored 198 goals in my first three full seasons with the Blues.

I'm always asked if I regret missing out on the Flames' Stanley Cup championship. The answer is always "No." I wanted to play, plain and simple. And the championship would not have meant anything, if I had been watching it from the press box.

It's absolutely uncanny how often my career path has lead to a fork in the road, and either I've made the right decision or it's been made for me.

First, Allie Cook directed me to Penticton. Then I chose Minnesota-Duluth, where Sertich skated me into NHL condition. I picked Brian Burke as my agent, and got a one-way contract when most players in my position don't.

Caron pulled me out of Calgary, and I found stardom in St. Louis. Burkie stepped down as my agent, and I ended up with Bob Goodenow, whose toughness helped me get a $7.1 million contract. I thought my world was ending when my centre, Peter Zezel, got traded. I ended up with Adam Oates. Remind me to buy a lottery ticket while my luck is holding up.

The championship that will be meaningful will be the one we win in St. Louis. When we win, I'll be as happy for Blues Chairman Mike Shanahan, President Jack Quinn and General Manager Ron Caron as I am for anyone. They have made a commitment to winning in St. Louis, and have backed it up with action.

They call Ron the Nutty Professor — but I don't see anything nutty about building a team that had the second-best record in hockey in 1990-91. After being hamstrung during Harry Ornest's ownership, Caron has finally been given the freedom, by Shanahan and Quinn, to do the job the way it should be done.

When player salaries were revealed for the first time, two years ago, a reporter wrote, "If you want to make money in the National Hockey League, don't meet me in St. Louis." The Blues had the league's lowest player payroll of $3.7 million.

Their philosophy now seems to be, "You get what you pay for." The Blues have some of the NHL's top salaries, because they have some the league's best players. Or, maybe they have some the league's best players because they pay some of the top salaries.

The Blues demonstrated their change in attitude by almost doubling their payroll in less than a year. When salaries were revealed in 1990-91, the Blues were among the NHL's big spenders, with a $6.7 million payroll. In 1989-90, Paul MacLean was our highest-paid player at $250,000. His salary increased to $270,000 for the 1990-91 season, and it was only the fifth-highest Blues' paycheque. We went from four to eleven players making more than $200,000 per season.

The players viewed the revamped pay structure as the Blues' commitment to bringing the Stanley Cup to St. Louis.

"Five or six years ago, being mediocre was enough in St. Louis," said Gino Cavallini, who has been with the Blues since 1985-86. "Not anymore."

All I know is Caron made me what I am today. He didn't develop me—but he jump-started my career.

He also made the trade to get Adam Oates, who is the National Hockey League's best passer this side of Gretzky.

Caron and Quinn also had enough backbone to buck the system, and sign Washington Capitals free agent Scott Stevens during the summer of 1990.

This summer, the Blues enraged the hockey world by signing young New Jersey Devils free-agent winger Brendan Shanahan, a young power forward with potential to be an All-Star.

Because Shanahan was a Type II free agent, under the age of twenty-four, compensation was determined by binding arbitration. That turned out to be the NHL's avenue to punish the Blues for being the only NHL team with the courage to actively pursue free agents.

Caron tried to work out a deal with the Devils' General Manager Lou Lamoriello, so it wouldn't have to go to arbitration. But Lamoriello clearly wanted to go to arbitration.

In a hearing with arbitrator Edward Houston in Toronto, the Blues argued that former first-round draft choice Rod Brind'Amour, plus goaltender Curtis Joseph and two draft choices, was adequate compensation for Shanahan. Lamoriello sought to acquire Stevens, who was also the Blues' captain.

In a fourteen-page decision, Houston awarded Stevens to New Jersey in what has to be one of the poorest arbitration decisions ever. There is no way you can justify Stevens being equal compensation for Shanahan. No offense to Shanahan, but you wouldn't consider trading Stevens for Shanahan. Stevens is one of the NHL's premier defensemen, and Shanahan hasn't yet peaked.

The Blues' offer was more than fair. Shanahan was picked second overall in the 1987 draft. Brind'Amour was taken ninth overall in 1988. Joseph had been a coveted college free agent two years before. Plus, the Blues were throwing in draft picks.

They say Houston knows his hockey; if he knew hockey he wouldn't make a decision like that.

It was a joke; it comes across like it was pre-ordained that the Blues would lose. It comes across like it was 'fixed,' to punish the Blues for failing to do what the other teams wanted them to do.

Maybe Stevens was being punished too, because he had the courage to defy the unwritten rule that players don't test free-agent waters. His move to the Blues helped trigger some of the NHL salary reform. When he was playing one of his first exhibition games with the Blues, Detroit Red Wings defenseman Brad McCrimmon skated next to him before a face-off, and said, "Congratulations on your contract." Players knew what Stevens had done for them.

Now he is a martyr. He loves St. Louis. The team wants him. But he has to leave, because a judge says he must.

I told every member of the media who would listen that Stevens should take his case to court, just like former Detroit Red Wings centre Dale McCourt did in 1977, when an arbitrator sent him to the Los Angeles Kings. McCourt lost in court, but by the time the decision came down, the Kings and Red Wings had agreed on other compensation.

The timing on this decision couldn't have been better for the players' association; it came as players were hammering out a new contract with owners. Nothing better points out how ridiculous the NHL free-agent system is than this ruling.

You have to admire Caron's guts. Other NHL general managers wanted to boil him in oil after he signed Stevens as a free agent. Boston Bruins General Manager Harry Sinden, forced to raise Ray Bourque's salary, to keep him in line with Stevens, joked that he would like to lob a hand grenade into the Blues' front office.

This past summer, the Chicago Blackhawks were unhappy because Ron made a contract offer to 'Hawks free agent Michel Goulet. The Blackhawks had called Caron during his negotiations, to warn him that they intended to match the offer. He told them, "We always operate within the rules. But I don't call other teams and ask them the best way to get their players."

Caron, who became Blues General Manager in 1983, is like Blues Coach Brian Sutter in his intense desire to win. Caron is a disciple of former Montreal Canadiens' legendary General Manager Sam Pollock, who assembled the Canadiens' dynasty in the 1970s. Caron was hired in 1968, and rose to chief scout in the Canadiens' organization.

He also coached the Canadiens' minor-league affiliate. Blues Assistant Coach Bob Berry remembers playing for him. "He had a burning desire to win," Berry recalled. "He could be hard to handle if we lost."

Now in his thirty-fifth NHL season, Caron never wavers on his conviction. After Houston's ruling took away his captain, Caron said, "Guess what? If I saw a chance to improve my team, I would do it again."

Caron doesn't get half the credit he deserves, mostly because he rocks the boat carrying all the owners. He doesn't sit around saying, "Gee, how can I make the league mad at me this summer?" He's just a man who loves to win; who loves to do his job aggressively. He doesn't say, "I'm not allowed to go after these guys, so I better not do it." The rules are there, and he takes advantage of them. Caron isn't trying to be George Steinbrenner, running around spending money for publicity's sake. The Blues aren't trying to buy the Stanley Cup; they are trying to win one, using all of the rules.

It's a joke that general managers are all mad at him. In baseball, general managers sign each other's players all the time, and they still get along. This is not a little game of Barbie and Ken, or G.I. Joe.

What I like most about Caron is his philosophy about management: "You can't win the Lotto unless you buy a ticket."

Caron once asked me to autograph a stick he could add to the many years of hockey memorabilia he had saved.

This is what I wrote: "To a man of vision, thanks, Brett Hull."

February 1982: Brett purchases his first suit to be best man at the wedding of Harry and Joanne Robinson: (left to right) Harry, Michelle, Brett, Joanne, Bart.

Brett receives one trophy at the Penticton Knights' awards banquet circa 1984...

...and another...

...and nine more, giving him a clean sweep.

Joanne and Brett at the Penticton banquet.

A mid-80s Christmas: Brett, Bart, Bob, Joanne, Blake, Michelle.

High school graduation: Brett with Shelley Marsh.

Brett, 19, playing golf in Florida.

Brett with Joanne and Harry at University of Minnesota-
Duluth Bulldogs' Parents Night circa 1985.

Brett enters the NHL, signing with the Calgary Flames in May 1986. (from left) Mike Sertich, Brett, Bob Johnson, Cliff Fletcher.

Harry, Brett, Mike Sertich at the signing in Calgary.

Brett at Bob Jr.'s wedding, July 1990.

The Brothers Hull: Bart, Blake, Brett, Bob.

Brett's sister
Michelle at Bob's
wedding.

The day after the wedding. (standing) Brett, Blake;
(seated) Michelle, Bob's wife Mardi, Bart.

CHAPTER 9

SUDSY

St. Louis Blues Coach Brian Sutter does smile. But you probably won't see it until the night we win the Stanley Cup championship.

You have to really work to get a laugh out of the man we call Sudsy. My best effort came during a practice, when a defenseman made an ill-advised play, and a stern-faced Brian began to lecture on the merits of flawless defensive play.

He had just hit the high note of his sermon, when his favorite non-defensive player raised his hand to make a point.

"What do you need, Hullie?"

"Brian, if you'd like, I'll go back and play some defense. I learned how to skate backwards over the summer."

The guys howled, and by all accounts, Sudsy produced what could be officially called a laugh. Actually, it was more of a groan.

Sudsy and I are nothing alike; he's one of the most intense hockey people I've ever met. I'm probably one of the least intense hockey players he's ever met.

"Brett," brother Blake always says to me, "the day you show some intensity will be the day the Doors' Jim Morrison comes back from the dead to play in concert."

Although Brian has a Type-A personality and I'm probably a Type-Z personality, our relationship couldn't be better. He understands that my carefree attitude doesn't translate into a lack of desire on the ice. And it may not be his way, but he appreciates that I play best when I'm having fun.

When Sudsy was hired to coach, he told me he wasn't interested in changing my style. He knows I can't be a Bob Gainey clone, a defensive disciple who covers his opponent closely enough to show up on his X-ray. Just being Brett Hull is difficult enough for me.

All Sudsy ever asks me to do is "improve each day as a player and a person." How can you argue with a coach who has that kind of philosophy? There's more to Sudsy than hockey.

When Brian was named coach of the Blues on June 20, 1988, at age thirty-one, it fulfilled the prophesy of the late Barclay Plager, who had been his mentor.

Plager, who died of brain cancer a few months before Sutter was named coach, repeatedly said Sutter was destined to coach the Blues. Brian was second on the Blues' all-time scoring list, and he was still playing effectively when he accepted the coaching position. He turned down the offer to be a player-coach, after thinking about Barclay's advice.

"He'd always tell me, 'Be proud of what you've done. Don't diminish it by staying around and playing a couple of extra years as a fourth-liner.'"

When he accepted the job, Sutter said the only regret he had was that Barclay hadn't lived to see it. "If he was here, he would have been the happiest guy in the room," Brian said.

My relationship with Brian was strengthened by a meeting after the 1988-89 season. After registering forty-one goals and forty-three assists in seventy-eight games, I was full of confidence as I walked into a meeting with Sudsy and assistant coach Bob Berry.

Sudsy made some general comments, then he looked at me with his most serious look.

"I don't want to insult you," he began. "But if you thought you were a good player last season, I hope you will think again."

Whoa! Hold on here. Didn't I just score forty-one goals? There are guys who play in this league for ten years and don't score forty-one goals. Brian Sutter was an excellent player, yet he only did it twice. Why are you getting on me? Why don't you criticize players who aren't producing?

Eventually, his theme hit home like an open-ice hip check. This wasn't Terry Crisp, asking me to change my personality and completely revamp my game. This was a coach who let me play the way I wanted to play. I was thinking, *Why don't I just shut up and listen to what he has to say.* After all, Sutter was only the best two-way hockey player in Blues history.

"You can come back and score forty-one goals again," he told me. "Or you can take the next step up and score sixty-five, and be a dominant NHL player. You can be a a lot better than you are."

He told me I had the same kind of goal-scoring knack as Mike Bossy. He wanted me to produce like the New York Islanders' Hall of Famer.

"I never ask anyone to give a hundred percent, because nobody knows what a hundred percent is," Brian said. "I just want my players to give me more than they gave yesterday. And tomorrow, I'll want more than you gave me today."

We talked about my role on the team, and how I needed to become more of a leader. That's difficult for me, because I'm not the kind of guy who can stand up in the dressing room and make a Knute Rockne-style plea for intensity.

"Everyone," Berry told me, "has to use what they have at their disposal. Bob Gainey was a quiet man, so he led the Montreal Canadiens simply by setting an example. You're a popular guy. Use that to the team's advantage."

I promised him I would make a better effort. We agreed that if I could report to training camp in the best shape of my life, it might be the boost I needed to become one the NHL's elite goal scorers.

In addition to the team aspects of his request, there was a financial incentive to have a great season. The contract I signed with the Flames expired. I needed a new deal. A few extra goals would be good for the team and help my cause in negotiations.

That summer, I went home and worked out with more dedication than ever before — not that I became the world's greatest devotee to fitness. Basically, I'm a lazy person. I hate running. Sometimes I put on running clothes at ten a.m. and don't get around to running until seven p.m. But I got it done. I showed up for training camp weighing 196 pounds — which left me almost emaciated by my standards.

A few pounds lighter, I got a few extra goals that season. Actually, I scored seventy-two goals, to break Jari Kurri's record for goals by a right winger.

"With as many chances as you've had," my centre, Peter Zezel, told me, "you probably should have scored a hundred goals."

The only question I've never been able to answer to anyone's satisfaction is why I'm able to score so many goals.

The truth is I have no idea. Scoring seventy-two goals seemed beyond my capability. Wayne Gretzky's record of ninety-two goals in a season seems like it would impossible to reach. That's why I don't set personal goals, and I don't ever think about anything except my next game. That's not some coaching mumbo-jumbo about taking one game at a time. That's just my recipe for staying loose and pressure-free. If I worry too much about what I'm trying to accomplish, I can't accomplish anything.

One piece of advice from Dad sums up my style. "Whenever you are the farthest away from the play," Dad would say, "that's when you are in it the most."

But this isn't a case of *Like Father, Like Son*. A good shot was the only part of Dad's package I inherited. Dad relied on speed and power; he roared down the ice like a high-calibre bullet. Dad was a express liner. I'm a freight train, just chugging along with short, choppy strides. I can't control the play like Wayne Gretzky or Mario Lemieux. I don't have great moves like Steve Yzerman. I need a good centre.

My style is to hang out in the weeds, blend in, look for an opening, slide in and hope someone gets me the puck.

What generally drives defenses nuts is that I have no game plan. Besides my shot, unpredictability is my best asset. It's difficult to check me, because I'm never quite sure myself what I'm going to do next. I don't carry the puck very often, and have no set pattern. I don't play a traditional style. For example, when our defense starts a breakout, I'll usually skate toward our zone, then loop back into the offensive zone as soon as I lose my checker.

The worst scoring situation for me is a break-away. I have too much time to think. The season I scored seventy-two, it seemed like I missed on seventy-two breakaways. My mind is the opposition's best friend. I'm thinking, *Should I shoot? How should I shoot? Should I deke first? Where should I shoot? When should I shoot?* By the time I determine what to do, I've lost the puck.

Over the years, teams have tried to shadow me. This means one player is assigned to follow me everywhere I go on the ice. Sometimes they will follow you right to the bench, to make sure you aren't going to jump back on the ice.

This hasn't proven to be all that effective, because I'm not exactly simple to shadow. First, I rarely carry the puck. Second, I never play the same way two shifts in a row. Finally, there are many ways to use a shadow to your advantage. If you skate toward another member of the opposition in front of the net, the opposing team suddenly finds itself with two of its players standing side-by-side. Usually when that happens, one of your teammates gets free.

I wasn't the first to be shadowed, and I certainly won't be the last. My dad was hounded mercilessly by some guys; it certainly didn't slow him down. A Red Wings player named Bryan Watson tailed Dad everywhere except at the hotel, when Dad went to Detroit. Dad doesn't even like to mention his name, "because he got enough publicity back when he was shadowing me."

The first guy to be serious about shadowing me was University of Denver forward Kermit Ecklebarger. He was a third-line forward, known more for defense than goal-scoring. He only had four or five goals all season, but he found another way to serve his team — by climbing into my pocket during a Western Collegiate Hockey Association playoff series, during my sophomore season at Minnesota-Duluth.

After one period of Ecklebarger following me end-to-end, coach Mike Sertich started his in-between-periods speech by addressing the situation.

"Brett, if you are planning to go to the bathroom between periods," Sertich said, "I think Ecklebarger is going to be in there handing you the toilet paper."

After the game, a reporter asked me what I thought about being shadowed.

"I think that's strange, because I'm not that good," I said.

Just as coach Rick Kozuback had done in Penticton, Sertich moved me back to defense on the power play, to get rid of Ecklebarger. Sertich says he was the only defender who bothered me during college. He only shadowed me for the two playoff games, and I scored in both of them.

Shadowing doesn't drive me crazy, because the Blues anticipate it. We scheme to make it work to our advantage. The only thing that bothered me about being shadowed by Minnesota North Stars' Gaetan Duchesne and Stewart Gavin in the playoffs last spring, was that we didn't work to take advantage of it.

My personal opinion on shadowing is that it's nuts. I believe coaches sometimes demean players by asking them to do it. If a coach wants a player to follow someone like he's a private detective, he should hire some high school kid. I mean no disrespect to the guys who do it, but it's an embarrassment to ask talented players to stand next to a goal-scorer for the entire game. If a coach ever asked me to shadow — and by that I mean total commitment to defense, without any regard to offense — I would refuse. I'm here to play hockey. The game is about skill, not harassment.

One myth about my scoring is that I score a ton of goals with a booming shot from outside the blue line.

Any goal I score from outside the blue line is an accident. Last season, I had one of those against the Chicago Blackhawks' Ed Belfour. I just was trying to hammer it into the Chicago zone, hoping a rebound might come out to Adam Oates. Belfour messed up. The puck went into the net. The legend of the Hull slap shot grows.

The opposition never cares how hard you can shoot the puck. All they are concerned about is from where. We'll let Montreal Canadiens right wing Stephane Richer shoot hundred-mile-an-hour slap shots the whole game, if he wants to crank them from beyond the blue line. Getting in position for a shot and a quick release are what is important to me.

Dad says he scored about fifty percent of his goals on a slap shot and fifty percent on his wrist shot. Probably only ten percent of my NHL goals have come on the slap shot. And all but a couple of those would be on the power play, when I've been on the point and had time for a full windup. My shot is the snap shot — all wrist, compact twenty-four-inch backswing, emphasis on accuracy. You don't have to be Arnold Swartzenegger to have a hard shot. It's like a golf swing, because it's all timing. The key is transfering your weight at precisely the right instant — causing the puck momentum and body momentum to work together in one direction. If you're shooting correctly, you should look graceful.

Two years ago, I also made an adjustment in my stick. I took the curve from the heel to the toe of the stick. I got that idea from watching guys like Mark Messier and Lanny McDonald. The toe curve gave them more snap on their shots — which is what I want out of my shot.

The shot is the glamour of scoring. It isn't really the most important part of the process. I think you need three things to be a top NHL scorer: First, you must have the ability to get open. If you can't find seams in the defense, you will never fire a clean shot.

Just as crucial, you need a centre who can get the puck at the right time. Offense is timing. Defense is disrupting timing. If a centre gets you the puck a second early, or a second late, it makes all the difference in the world. Finally, you need luck. Anyone who says you can be a fifty-goal scorer without luck is nuts.

Another myth about my scoring is that I've produced more in St. Louis because I've lost weight. Actually, I weigh the same as I did in Calgary. And because my weight fluctuates like shares on the New York Stock Exchange, there were times during my eighty-six-goal season that I played heavier than I was in Calgary. But I will confess that I'm more concerned about my weight than I was earlier in my career. My body fat is lower than it was in Calgary. By the way, I hate players who can eat from now until Tuesday without gaining a pound.

Sudsy's weight probably never changed more than an ounce either way during the twelve seasons he played for the Blues. Sudsy doesn't bother me much about my weight; he has the assistant coaches do it. But when Sudsy talks, we listen. We know if anyone can take us to the Stanley Cup, it's this guy. He wants to win so badly it pains him. In his first three seasons, the Blues' point totals rose from 78 in 1988-89, to 83 in 1989-90 and to 105 in 1990-91. At age thirty-four, he was the youngest person ever to win NHL Coach of the Year. Red Berenson was the only other Blues coach to win the honor.

Before the Blues decided to hire Sudsy in 1988, they talked to Mike Keenan, who had been fired by the Philadelphia Flyers. After talking to the Blues, Keenan decided to join the Chicago Blackhawks. Can you imagine how different my career might have been if Keenan was my coach?

There actually was some criticism of the Blues for choosing a player to coach, instead of recycling one of the established coaches. Now, I can't even imagine the Blues without Sutter behind the bench. The players feel fortunate to have him.

I find it interesting that seventy-five or eighty percent of the players in this league dislike their coaches. I hear the Canadiens like Pat Burns, and Doug Risebrough is well-received by the Calgary Flames. And the Maple Leafs think Tom Watt's all right. There probably are a couple of others who get along well with players. But as a group, NHL coaches aren't winning any popularity contests with their players. All I'm saying is that it makes you wonder.

Sudsy never talks to me about scoring goals. Yet he has his way of motivating me. At one point last season, I scored five goals in three games. He told reporters he didn't think I was hot. He expected me to do that, he insisted.

He agreed that he would consider ten goals in three games to be a hot streak for yours truly. *St. Louis Post-Dispatch* writer Tom Wheatley asked me what I thought of Sudsy's ideas about my goal scoring.

"What do I think? I think I would have to be an idiot to comment on something like that," I said.

Sudsy and I played together for part of one season. He knows what I can do offensively. He just leaves my offensive play alone. Defensively, he has changed me. "Defense is an attitude, not an ability," he tells me regularly. I've started to believe that.

Sudsy has mellowed ever so slightly over the past three seasons — but I'm not going to be the one to tell him that. Brian has such great desire to win that sometimes he just boils over.

Two seasons ago, we were in Los Angeles for a game against the Kings. Wayne Gretzky and Bernie Nicholls were both out of the lineup with injuries, but the Kings smoked us, 9-3. We were so brutal the Kings had us down, 4-0, before we even knew we were playing. It was so bad that Marty McSorley, who isn't exactly a threat to win the scoring title, scored two goals and had one assist. He was named the Number One star. One of his goals was even short-handed. I didn't get a point, and was on the ice for three Kings' goals. We stunk like the dead fish at Redondo Beach.

When Brian came into the room after the game his face was an angry red, as though he had fallen asleep for ten hours under a sun lamp. Linemate Sergio Momesso leaned over to forward Kelly Chase and me, and said, "I think we should all probably keep our helmets on for this one."

Sergio was right. Brian started out by telling us how embarrassing our performance was, then he exploded like a keg of TNT. He trashed the place. It was a Hall of Fame tirade. During his grand finale, he shattered Paul Cavallini's stick over a stall.

Brian Sutter's will to win is second to none. That's the trademark of the Sutter family, fromViking, Alberta. None of his five brothers who played or play in the NHL have much tolerence for losing, either. When the Blues play against Ron Sutter of the Philadelphia Flyers, or Brent Sutter of the New York Islanders, Brian doesn't even acknowledge he has brothers on the ice. Socializing, he says, is for the summer. I'm telling you, Brian Sutter wants to win more than anyone I've met.

One time, two years ago, Brian was so mad at us that he wanted to take on the whole team.

"You guys think you're so tough," he bellowed. "Why don't I take five of you guys into the next room. We'll turn off the lights. We'll see who walks out of the room."

After Sudsy stalked off, Craig Coxe, one of our tough guys, said, "No way would I ever go into a room with him."

Chase, who we call Chaser, probably should have gotten the award last season for getting the best smile out of Sudsy.

It happened in a game against the Chicago Blackhawks, when Kelly and Wayne Van Dorp were in the traditional exchange of insults that is the precurser to any major bout.

"C'mon, Wayne, show us the new trick you learned," Kelly said. "Show us how you learned to turn left over the summer."

Van Dorp, by then, had blood in his eyes. He called Kelly something that was derogatory to several members of his family.

"I'll bet you have no idea how to spell that," Kelly said.

According to eyewitnesses, Sudsy put his head down to prevent the world from seeing he was laughing his tail off.

ST. LOUIS

CHAPTER 10

PIZZA
WITH
EXTRA
DOUGH

Philadelphia Flyers defenseman Mark Howe tells the story about the toughest player he ever saw, who didn't make the NHL.

He was a centre, and played with Howe on the Detroit Junior Red Wings. It was the U.S. National Junior Tournament in San Diego, 1970. A high stick catches this guy. An eye socket is crushed. Blood everywhere. He's toast. But when teammates rush over, he's struggling to get up. He insists he's going to play. Trainers and coaches have to order him off the ice. The damage was so severe he needed plastic surgery.

The centre's name was Bob Goodenow. He was my agent during one of the most difficult contract negotiations in NHL history. When your future is at stake, you want a guy like Goodenow. It's like having Norman Swartzkopf leading your charge. That's why players chose him as the executive director of the players' association. He's a tough, experienced fighter, and he doesn't mind getting bloodied if he believes in the cause.

Burkie told me as much in 1987, when he gave up his agent business to become director of hockey operations for the Vancouver Canucks. He lobbied for his partner, Goodenow, to replace him. "He's smart, and he's tough," Burkie said. "If I had a son ready to play hockey, I would want Bob as his agent."

Goodenow, from the Detroit suburb of Dearborn, used to hang out with Gordie Howe's family. He played ball hockey with sons Mark and Marty in the Howe driveway. He ended up captain of the Harvard team, and played for the U.S. national team in the World Championships in 1974.

The Washington Capitals gave him a look, but it was one of those we've-already-decided-you-can't-make-it tryouts. For my sake, it was a blessing he didn't make it. When he saw he had no future, he went to law school and became an agent.

Burkie remembered playing against Goodenow in college.

"He was one tough customer, and he was a good player," Burkie said. "He was belligerent, and that wasn't Harvard's trademark. He was their mini-goon. He has more credibility with general managers, because he knows the game."

Toughness is a small part of Goodenow's total package: he's shrewd, manipulative and a master planner. He prepares like he's readying for an assault on Kuwait. If Bob didn't wear such a godawful, brutal, unstylish London Fog overcoat, he would be among the coolest guys I know.

Looking back on my nine months of negotiations, it's easy to say the Blues could have saved plenty by signing me earlier. But who knew I was going to score seventy-two goals? Certainly not me. Each goal I scored put more and more pressure on the Blues. They figured I had to cool off. I didn't. Here's how I looked at it: Blues President Jack Quinn and General Manager Ron Caron were always trying to make the right business decision for the Blues. That meant they had to keep an eye on the bottom line. Bob was always trying to do what was best for me. Eventually, we realized those weren't mutually exclusive concerns.

There were hard feelings at times. Both sides grew frustrated. But it's like the Stanley Cup final. Two teams beat on each other for ten days. Yet when it's over, you line up, shake hands and say, *It was a heckuva of a battle.* That's what happened when I finally signed a contract. We shook hands and said it had been a heckuva battle.

Truth is, I wanted to stay with the Blues all along. They had been great to me. I liked the team. I liked the city. I liked the fans, and I liked management. I respect Quinn's efforts to make the team better, and Caron rescued me from the Calgary press box. For that, I'll be forever grateful.

But I didn't like them enough to accept their first contract offer on August 10, 1989. In a three-year deal, they wanted to give me yearly salaries of $145,000, $165,000 and $165,000.

Remember, I'd just come off a season of forty-one goals and eighty-four points, and I was making $125,000, entering my option year. The amazing aspect of that offer was that I wasn't all that upset. Bob and I figured the Blues were trying to prod me. In initial talks, Bob was selling me as one of the league's top right wings, and Caron would only grudgingly concede I was in the top twenty. One of his first notes to Bob compared me to Cam Neely,

Kevin Dineen, Gary Leeman and so on. The list included just about everyone except Eddie Shack.

"I am ready to pay for some higher achievements," Caron told Bob. "If he has a hundred points and is a plus player, then we would consider a hundred-percent increase."

On September 12, Goodenow faxed a counter-offer to the Blues that was as welcome as a Scud missile. He said I'd sign for one year, plus an option year, for $250,000, with a bonus package that included $10,000 for thirty goals, $10,000 more for forty-five and $30,000 for fifty goals.

Two days later, Caron tersely answered the fax. "I'm shocked."

A week later, the Blues offered four years at $150,000, $160,000, $170,000 and $170,000. We were getting nowhere, Bob told me. The symbolic start of the contract war came when I had to write a check for $4,500, to pay disability insurance premiums to cover my option year. That expense took my checking account a little too close to zero to suit my fiscally conservative nature.

"Are you sure I need to do this?" I asked again, pen in hand.

Bob gave me one of those get-your-stuff-together-and-trust-me looks. So I stopped talking and started writing.

The funny part was that the insurer had the same perspective as the Blues. I couldn't get a $1 million policy, because my career wasn't considered to be worth that much.

Even at that point, I was thinking I'd end up signing for about $250,000 to $300,000 a year. But Bob wasn't thinking that — especially when every shot started going in. I scored eleven goals in my first ten games, and seventeen in the first twenty.

By Christmas, I had thirty-one goals in thirty-six games. "You're on a roll," Bob declared. "I think we ought to run with it."

So we did. By then, the media had begun to speculate about my chances on the free-agent market. I was a Type II free agent, which meant a team signing me faced the compensation price of two first-round picks in the top seven to sign me, or as many as five over five years, if they weren't in the top seven.

There was speculation that the Detroit Red Wings and Chicago Blackhawks might try to sign me. Both were looking for scoring wingers, and Chicago, of course, had some familiarity with the Hull name.

On December 12, the *Detroit News* printed a ridiculous rumor that the Blues were considering trading me back to Calgary, in a deal involving Gary Suter. What a joke.

Goodenow decided to have some fun. He copied the story and mailed it to Flames General Manager Cliff Fletcher, with a note: "Will you be calling me? Merry Christmas, Bob."

To be truthful, I never thought any team would sign me. But that didn't stop me from putting my house on the market in January. It sold in a couple of months.

Michael Gobuty, who was trying to start the Global Hockey League then, called Goodenow. He was talking about making me the highest-paid player in professional hockey. I never even seriously considered his offer. Even if I believed this Global thing would make it, I would never have jumped. My dad has awesome statistics — 913 goals in 23 seasons in the NHL and World Hockey Association. Yet I think he doesn't get the credit he deserves, because some of those goals came in the WHA. I didn't want that to happen to me. To the NHL, Dad still has 610 goals, which is the total he had in 15 NHL seasons. Maybe if I was late in my career it would have been an option. But not then.

My hottest streak of the season came from December 30 to February 13, when I had a twenty-game point-scoring streak. With twenty-one goals and fifteen assists during that span, I truly was on a roll.

This success put more heat on the Blues. They offered $200,000, $250,000, $300,000, $325,000 for three years, plus an option year.

Bob called me on January 10, and told me he was going to send the Blues a fax stating that our starting point was $600,000, $700,000 and $800,000, plus bonuses for three years.

That signaled a cold war that lasted for thirty days. We heard nothing. No counter-offer. No rejection. Nothing.

While the Blues did nothing, Bob upped the ante again. We were having dinner at Greek Town in Detroit, and we were each scribbling figures on our placemats as we talked about our plans. Finally, Bob jotted down a figure and put his hand over it. "This is what we have to go for now," Bob said.

I stared at the figure quietly. I counted the six zeroes twice. I couldn't even say the number.

The idea of being a million-dollar man was too unbelievable to comprehend. Finally, I spoke. My response, of course, was brilliant. "Are you sure I'm worth that?" I said.

Bob just laughed. The battle plan was set.

Days later, he broke the news to Blues Chairman Michael Shanahan and Quinn, over a February lunch in Toronto. He told me they didn't react much, just chewed his words like they were croutons on the luncheon salad.

We didn't hear from the Blues for a while. By that time, I was thinking we probably shouldn't continue negotiating until after the season. On March 2, I had scored twice and added two assists in a 5-4 win against the Islanders. I had sixty-seven goals in sixty-seven games, and I had just joined Bernie Federko and Doug Gilmour as the only Blues players to net more than a hundred points in a season.

At this point, Bob was thinking we needed more than $1 million. That was why he sounded confused, when he called a week later.

"Have you changed agents?"

"Not that I know of."

"Quinn just called me, and said you were willing to sign for a million a year."

"I haven't talked to Mr. Quinn."

"Well, your mom has been negotiating with him."

We laughed. Obviously, Mom was worrying again.

Mom actually did play a role in the negotiations. Coincidentally, each time she would call Jack Quinn to check on the status of negotiations, we were at a point of high frustration. Her calls were like a cease-fire during the battle. She reassured Quinn that I really wanted to remain with the Blues.

"Your mom was a great morale booster," Quinn later remarked. "Her timing was uncanny. She probably only called four times, but she would call right when I needed a boost. Maybe she was just being intuitive. Maybe she could sense that we were on the edge. But she would call and tell me, 'Bob's really a good guy, and Brett's a good guy. He'll sign. Just keep working at it.'"

A week or so later, the Blues sent another offer. It was a five-year deal with most of the money tied into bonuses. It was so complex that they sent along a computer printout to spell out exactly what I would earn if I achieved certain levels of performance. The bottom line: if I scored fifty goals and more than one hundred points, was a plus player and brushed my teeth every day, I could earn $1.2 million the first year and more than $2 million the last year.

Clearly, the Blues were getting very serious. But we didn't embrace the proposal, because it was too dependent upon bonuses. The base salary was only about $350,000.

Goodenow told Quinn that he couldn't sell the package to me. Quinn was very unhappy.

"What do you mean, you can't sell a million-dollar-a-year offer?" Quinn said.

Bob countered with a two years-plus-one offer at more than $1 million a season, plus a signing bonus of $500,000. Quinn rejected the counter-offer. "As a responsible member of management, I don't want to give a million-dollar raise," he said.

After I finished the season with a record of seventy-two goals by a right wing, the pressure on the Blues intensified. We knew sports history in St. Louis also was in our favor. The St. Louis Cardinals baseball team had allowed Jack Clark to sign with the Yankees. No one stepped forward to prevent the National Football League Cardinals from moving to Phoenix. Fans are still angry about those losses, and it was pretty clear there would be a backlash against the Blues if I didn't sign.

Letters to the editor and callers to local talk shows were clear on their message: sign Brett Hull. Season-ticket holders were writing to say they would buy more tickets if the Blues signed me, or cancel their existing order if they didn't.

Quinn joked that even his daughter, Connie, who went to school with me in Vancouver, was on him to sign me.

"I'd hear it all day at the office, or when I'd go to the bank, or to the store. 'When are you going to sign Hull?'," Quinn told me later. "Then I'd come home, and Connie would say, 'Aw c'mon, Dad, Brett is such a nice guy. Sign him.'"

Susie Mathieu, Blues vice-president of marketing and public relations, is among my closest friends. She handles everything in my hockey life; she organizes my appearances, sorts out my fan mail and has given me good advice many times. She even went to my house once and changed the cat litter. She probably is the most valuable player in the Blues organization. If she left, the whole team would fall apart. Even she got pressure on the home front.

"My six-year-old son, Joey, came up to me," Susie told me, "and he says if we don't sign you, I have to move out of the house."

The Blues' last contract offer had at least made it clear that we were, at last, negotiating in the same financial neighborhood. But it was June before negotiations continued. By then, the situation was getting critical, as far they were concerned. On June 31, I would become a free agent. Time was my ally and the Blues' enemy.

Bob doesn't usually take clients into negotiations, but he said he wanted me in on this round. He felt my presence would bring the meeting to a conclusion — one way or the other. We met at Norwood Country Club in suburban St. Louis on a Friday night, and it didn't go particularly well. Bob had laid out a three-plus-one contract, and a four-plus-one, and we had asked them to pick one. They had tried to compare my contract to Detroit Red Wings centre Steve Yzerman's contract. Bob was having none of that.

There was little movement. When we broke off talks, there wasn't much optimism, except that we agreed to meet the next morning in the Blues' office.

It was a crazy night. My girlfriend, Alison, and Susie had been waiting at my house, and when we didn't get home right away, they decided to go out. Because I had no keys to the house, they left the door open.

My neighbor then came home, saw my door open, and did the neighborly thing of locking up my house.

Caron had brought us home. When we couldn't get in, we decided we would go the Train Wreck bar in the St. Louis suburb of Rock Hill. The Train Wreck is an excellent place. An electric train runs around the perimeter of the bar. The clientele is a mixture of young professionals and blue collars. Softball teams go there. It's a classic neighborhood bar. It reminds me of the bars back in Duluth.

It certainly wasn't the kind of bar Ron Caron usually goes to. But he stayed until last call, and I think he had a good time. We may have been on opposite sides of the negotiating table, but thankfully, Ron and I never took it personally.

Three months before, Caron had endured nine hours of flight complications to get to Toronto, to see me break Dave Babych's Blues record of fifty-two goals. I had fifty-one, going into a Saturday game against Toronto. We fell behind, 1-0, and I scored a hat trick to break the record. We won, 7-1.

Caron was in the dressing room after the game. Inclement weather caused him flight misery — nine hours to get from Detroit to Toronto. It's usually an hour-long flight. He congratulated me and gave me a $200 bottle of champagne. "It's an '82 Krug," Caron said. "It's the best champagne I own." I told him I would keep it for a special occasion. Unknown to me, such an occasion was rapidly approaching.

Alison and Susie had found us at the Train Wreck. After it closed, we were invited to a friend's house to continue the evening.

In between bites of a roast beef sandwich, I remember Bob telling Susie he didn't think the Blues were going to be able to sign me the next morning.

"You're forcing us to test the free agent market," he said.

Instead of heading home at two a.m., we found ourselves arriving at my door just before dawn.

The next morning, I discovered that 250-pound Duluth bear inside my head. The meeting was scheduled for eleven a.m., but I wasn't worried because I thought Susie was supposed to pick us up. As usual, I was confused. The phone rang about noon. It was Susie.

"Where are you guys?" she said. "Ron and Jack are here. I think they're worried you aren't coming."

The day's emotional ride began in earnest. Bob and I huddled in Caron's office, and Quinn and

Caron huddled in Quinn's office. We would negotiate. Separate. Negotiate. Separate.

At one point, Bob was ticked because he felt the Blues were trying to take back some point they had already conceded. He came out of the office, walked up to Suzie and said, "What airline do I call to get a flight to Chicago?"

A few minutes later, I came out and told her, "Don't worry. Call Joey and tell him you won't have to move out of the house."

There were several swings as we tried to talk about bonus clauses and incentives. Finally, Bob and I decided we needed to get away and talk. We announced we were leaving.

"You are coming back, aren't you?" Caron asked.

We were coming back. But we had no idea what we were going to do until we entered Imo's Pizzeria, down the road from the arena. We ordered what turned out to be a million-dollar pizza, which comes with everything on it.

While munching pizza, the two of us decided I would sign if the Blues would give me a package of about $7 million. That meant we were only about $1 million apart, and we both knew it could be worked out.

We returned to Quinn's office, and negotiations started to progress more smoothly. I got a country-club membership and the use of a car. They agreed to Bob's insistence that I get a $25,000 bonus for every home playoff game. Bob had pretty much thought of everything. If I hadn't owned every Neil Young album, he would have gotten them to throw that in, too.

We even got a clause that reopens negotiations when the Blues win the Stanley Cup. Notice I say *when*, and not *if*.

The final deal was four years: $600,000 to sign, plus yearly salaries of $1,166,000, $1.5 million, $1.6 million and $2.2 million. The total was $7.1 million. In addition, there was an elaborate bonus section that covered everything except my singing in the dressing room.

Mom and Brian Sutter were among the first people I called. When I got in touch with Bobby Jr., he was amused at how the contract linked Dad and me.

"He was the one who escalated the salaries in the 1970s, and you are doing it in the 1990s," he stated.

My dad had signed a ten-year contract with the Winnipeg Jets for $2.75 million in 1971, including a $1 million signing bonus. He had a thirty-nine-page contract, which shows how careful he was to protect himself. He wanted to make sure he got paid — even if the team, or league, didn't make it.

Perhaps there is some correlation, but I didn't consider myself a maverick. I wasn't trying to become famous as the player who started salaries on the upward spiral. Let's not forget Wayne Gretzky was making $3 million a year, and Lemieux $2 million, when I signed for an average of about $1.75 million a season.

But Bob and I did get fired up when we talked about my contract's possible impact on the rest of league. We knew how underpaid some of the NHL's stars were, because the Blues used those woefully low salaries as justification for not paying me what I wanted. They would point out that Messier was only making slightly less than a $1 million and Bourque was earning about $400,000.

Bob, who loves the game as much as anyone I know, was particularly vocal about the league's salary structure. He was hotter than the Cajun seafood we were eating at S&P Oyster Bar, on Manchester in St. Louis. It seemed like we ended up there every time he came to town. In between bites of gumbo and oysters, we would take a bite out of the salary structure.

"If we get what we want," Bob said, "we'll help guys like Messier, Bourque and others get what they have deserved for years."

At the start of the next season, I was standing in the face-off circle in a game against Boston, and Bourque skated by me.

"Congratulations on the contract," Bourque said. "It's good for all of us."

One more thing about Bob Goodenow: he is player's friend, when it comes to fees. Most agents charge five-percent commission for negotiating your contract. Bob charged by the hour, and I think he stopped counting about halfway through our negotiation.

Under a five-percent-commission agent, I would have paid at least $350,000 for my new contract. Bob's bill was about $60,000.

There was a great sense of relief in the Blues office after I signed. Pure elation. Handshakes all around. There was a football on Quinn's desk, and we started throwing it around. Caron threw wildly, and I made a window-saving snag.

"Never a doubt," I said.

"Just like this contract." Caron said. We laughed.

I opened Caron's champagne that night. Michael Shanahan held the press conference at his house. Everyone got a chance to speak. When Caron's turn came, he started talking about my potential. He said the NHL expansion to San Jose in 1991-92, and two other sites a year later, would dilute the talent. He talked about how expansion can play havoc with goaltending depth around the league. He predicted I might be able to score a hundred goals in a season. Maybe the champagne went to his head.

ST. LOUIS

CHAPTER 11

FEAR

OF

FAMINE

Every day I wake up scared to death I'm never going to score another goal. Entering the 1990-91 season, I was more terrified than usual.

Scoring goals is my talent; I don't do anything well except fill the net. I figure if goals stop coming, I'll be going. Some players have scored forty or fifty goals, then never found their scoring touch again. Plus, I had this staggering contract, and kept envisioning every checker in the NHL salivating for a chance to make me look like a slug. My nightmare was thinking about what life would be like if I started the season slowly.

The seventy-two goals I scored in 1989-90 hadn't eased my fears. I really believed Peter Zezel was the main reason I was the NHL's leading goal scorer. He was an top centre with a special knack for getting the puck to me.

When Zezel trade rumors swirled in the spring of 1990, I told my agent, Bob Goodenow, to tell Caron I wouldn't sign if the Blues dealt Zezel.

"We're not planning to trade Zezel," Caron told Bob.

Two weeks after my contract was signed, Zezel and Mike Lalor were sent to the Washington Capitals for Geoff Courtnall. So much for my career as an assistant general manager.

I expected bad press in 1990-91. I figured any time I didn't score, someone would be thinking, *Seven million for him? He's not worth it.* Of course, there was always a chance I could score seventy-two goals again. But it seemed rather unlikely. Only Wayne Gretzky (ninety-two in 1981-82, eighty-seven in 1983-84, and seventy-three in 1984-85), Phil Esposito (seventy-six in 1970-71) and Mario Lemieux (eighty-five in 1988-89) had scored as many as seventy-two goals in one season in the NHL. Dad, of course, had seventy-seven for the Jets, in the WHA.

The upbeat mood at training camp helped reduce — though not eliminate — some of my fears. There was a great sense of anticipation about the Blues; fans were talking about the Blues competing for the Stanley Cup. My four-year contract had been front page news in St. Louis. Signing free agent Scott Stevens had raised optimism even more. There was more interest in Blues hockey than at any other time in the franchise's twenty-four-year history. Remember, this was a franchise that came close to packing up and moving to Saskatoon. In early 1983, Ralston-Purina negotiated an agreement to sell the team to a Saskatoon-based group, headed by Bill Hunter.

The NHL wouldn't approve moving the franchise. Ralston-Purina filed an anti-trust lawsuit; the NHL countersued. On May 13, Ralston-Purina fired Blues employees and told NHL President John Ziegler that the franchise was now in the league's hands. When the June draft came, the Blues' spot in the order was simply bypassed.

Meanwhile, community interest in the team all but disappeared. When Harry Ornest bought the team, in July of that year, he inherited a season-ticket base of 5,300. All that remained was the hard-core faithful. It was an uphill fight for the Blues, not helped by missing out on a year's supply of draft picks.

The franchise didn't turn the corner until Michael Shanahan became general partner on December 13, 1986.

He is the chairman and majority stockholder of Engineered Support Systems, a 430-employee company, which makes support equipment for the defense industry. His company manufactured items such as air conditioners for airplanes and water purification systems for U.S. troops in the Persian Gulf war.

Shanahan is a very likable guy with great people skills. And you have to like anyone who asks a builder to drill a hole into his basement floor, so he can practice his putting. In my next house, that's a must.

He has a great sense of humor. When he attends meetings of the NHL Board of Governors, he playfully jabs NHL vice-presidents Brian O'Neill and Jim Gregory about the quality of NHL officiating. He jokingly complains that, no matter what aspect of officiating you discuss, the official league response is always "It all evens out."

With that in mind, Shanahan ordered three high-quality sweaters with the words *It all evens out* sewn on the front. He sent one each to O'Neill, Gregory and

Bryan Lewis, who is the supervisor of officials. Apparently, they loved the joke and the sweaters.

Unlike the previous owner, Shanahan was willing to spend some money; he gave Quinn and Caron the freedom to be bold. It was Shanahan who told Quinn to recall Caron from a Fourth of July fishing trip, and sign Stevens. Fans showed their appreciation through ticket purchases.

To those who had been around during the Ralston-Purina and Ornest years, it seemed like a miracle when season-ticket sales jumped from 9,100 to 12,500. Ron Caron joked that he signed seven autographs in his first seven years in St. Louis, then signed more than seven hundred at one charity breakfast, during the 1990-91 training camp. Going into the 1991-92 season, the Blues season-ticket base was 13,900 and counting.

During training camp, I decided I wanted to go out and prove that owners didn't have to sit on their wallets all the time. I wanted to stick it to the teams criticizing the Blues for spending big bucks to sign Stevens and me.

Probably, I should have been worried about how my relationship with my teammates would change, now that I had become one of the NHL's highest-paid players. But I didn't assume that it would change. I was right.

Sergio Momesso, my linemate the previous season, told me not to worry. "Whether you earn $100,000 or $1 million, you'll be the same," he told me.

I should have known he wouldn't stop there.

"You're still as arrogant as ever," he joked.

Everything was the same. Kelly Chase, Ron Wilson, Dave Lowry and Gino Cavallini were still playing cards. The official Blues' game is Snarples, which was invented by Harold Snepsts. Need I say more?

Bob Berry, Paul MacLean and I were still doing the daily *USA TODAY* crosswords. The conversation always takes on a cerebral quality during the crossword hour.

"Bob, did you get 43 across?"

"Of course I did, you stupe."

"What's the answer?"

"I'm not telling you."

"Hey, Bob, you're a horse's rear end."

"Thank you"

Crosswords are actually something of a hockey tradition. Bob Berry picked up the habit from former NHLer Parker MacDonald, who was an assistant coach with the Los Angeles Kings. Parker told Berry that Gordie Howe used to do them regularly, when he played with the Red Wings.

Berry is superior at crosswords. "But's it's only because you've been around longer than I have," I tell him. "Of course, you're going to know more stuff."

On the day our first paycheques arrived in October, I knew there would be no problems with the guys accepting my new income. When the paycheques were distributed, I realized that all the guys were staring at me. They all had big grins on their faces.

"Well, how much is it?" Momesso said.

So we had the ceremonial opening of the Hullie's first cheque under his new contract. We get paid twice a month. Even I didn't know for sure how much it would be.

The envelope, please. *SIXTY THOUSAND DOLLARS!* Even I was startled.

"I don't even want to think about how long it takes me to earn that much money," Trainer Mike Folga said.

After that, the jokes were at my expense. Take that literally. Every day in practice, guys kept telling Assistant Coach Bob Berry that they wanted to be my centre, because I was obligated to buy lunch for my linemates.

During my seventy-two-goal season, I developed more confidence in telling my ideas to the coaches. Guys were always hooting on me about how much time I was spending with the coaching staff.

The coaches' office had the names of all the assistants printed on the door. Someone wrote *Brett Hull* on a piece of tape, and stuck it on the door under the names of the other assistant coaches. We had a lot of fun in that training camp.

Fear gripped me again, when the season began. I wondered how I ever scored seventy-two goals the season before. The fear began to leave after I scored seven goals in my first seven games, then thirteen in ten games, then sixteen in thirteen games and twenty-two in twenty-one games. When I had back-to-back hat tricks in a home-and-home series against the Toronto Maple Leafs, I knew there wouldn't be any problems scoring goals.

Remember, this was before I was playing on a line with Adam Oates. For the first quarter of the season, I only played with Adam regularly on the power play. Then, Oates tore an abdominal muscle and missed eighteen games, from November 3 until December 16.

Caron insists that the first two months of the season, when I played with several different linemates, was important for my confidence. "The Peter Zezel syndrome took on a smaller dimension," he says. All I still know is that Peter was a big part of my seventy-two-goal season.

The media crush was even heavier than it had been the year before. Every time I would be sitting down, talking to a reporter or staring into a television camera, teammates would walk by and roll their eyes. Or better still, they would interject their opinions on whatever subject I happened to be talking about. I love that about hockey. No one allows anyone to be too serious about anything but playing the game.

"Brett's like *The Natural*," Dave Lowry told *St. Louis Post-Dispatch* reporter Dave Luecking. "Robert

Redford is going to play him next." I didn't know whether to take that as a compliment or a zing. Either way, I liked it.

Bob Goodenow, my agent, told reporters he had never seen a career take such a dramatic jump to a higher level.

"The only thing I can equate it to," Bob told reporters, "is Cecil Fielder hitting fifty-one home runs for the Detroit Tigers in 1990. He was a decent power-hitter, then all of the sudden, he's the first American Leaguer to hit more than fifty home runs since Roger Maris and Mickey Mantle did it, in 1961."

There's something about baseball comparisons that appeals to hockey people. No one likes them better than Caron, whose not-so-secret dream is to be a major league baseball scout after he retires from hockey. As a youngster in Hull, Quebec, he played baseball more than hockey. He changed positions, from catcher to pitcher, "because I took too many foul tips without wearing a mask".

"But the closest I ever got to the major leagues," Caron said, "was sitting three rows behind the Baltimore Orioles, at a game in the Toronto SkyDome."

His favorite team was the New York Yankees. Now, he follows the St. Louis Cardinals, Toronto Blue Jays and Cincinnati Reds. Jack Quinn's brother, Bob, runs the Reds' organization.

Walk into Caron's office near the end of hockey season, and you'll probably receive an earful of Ron's spring training diamond notes. He'll tell the story of deciding not to draft Massachusetts prep hockey star Tom Glavine, after investigating his baseball talent. As soon as Caron discovered Glavine was a pro-prospect left-handed pitcher, he removed him from the Blues' draft list. He knew major league baseball wouldn't allow a left-handed pitcher to skate away to hockey. Glavine was drafted by the Los Angeles Kings, and signed with the Atlanta Braves.

After the Kings plucked Glavine, Caron told Vachon that, if Glavine played in the NHL, he would become the league's first one-armed player.

"He looked at me funny," Caron remembered. "I told him, 'The only way he would give up baseball, is if he loses his left arm.'"

If you have time to listen, Caron will tell you tales about how Hall of Fame defenseman Doug Harvey was a two-sport star, long before Bo Jackson was splitting his time between Kansas City and Hollywood.

"Harvey was the top hitter in the Border League in 1947, playing for the Ottawa Nationals," Caron said. "He won the batting championship, and moved to the Montreal Canadiens right after that. I think he even played AAA a little later."

Now that you understand Caron's love of baseball, I can explain about one of the nicest compliments I have ever received.

On November 13, we played the last-place Quebec Nordiques. We were trying to win our fifth game in a row, and the score was tied 2-2 with less than two minutes left in regulation, when Nordiques centre Joe Sakic banged a shot off the crossbar and the puck came down-ice in a hurry. A rebound came to me at the corner of the net, with goaltender Ron Tugnutt in front of me. There was absolutely no room. He had the angle. I waited and waited. Tugnutt didn't flinch. Finally, I flicked it upstairs. Somehow, the puck got in for the game-winner at 18:46. After an empty-net-ter, we won 4-2.

"It was like watching Mickey Mantle hit the ball 565 feet at Griffith Stadium in Washington, in 1952," Caron told a reporter. "That goal will always be vivid in my memory. From that position, only a guy like Hull, Mario Lemieux or Gretzky could score it."

Another key goal came on January 29, against Buffalo. At 4:15 of overtime, Oatsie won the draw and fed me at the top of the circle. The wrister went clean into the net.

Kelly Chase told me, after that goal, that I needed a raise. "Just one more goal for the fat boy," I said.

On February 17, the Blues were in Calgary. At that point, I had 182 goals in 227 games — the equivalent of about three full seasons — with the Blues. Fletcher, at the time of the trade, said I might score 180 over the next four seasons. I added my sixty-second and sixty-third goals of the season against the Flames. The *Calgary Sun* ran a cartoon depicting a blushing Cliff Fletcher holding an empty Hull sweater, and saying "Oops." It was amusing.

That was in the middle of my best goal-scoring streak of the season. I had at least one goal in thirteen consecutive games I played in from January 22 to February 23. I wasn't blanked until visiting Chicago on February 24.

The NHL record for a consecutive goal-scoring streak is sixteen, by Harry (Punch) Broadbent of Ottawa, in 1921-22. Second was Montreal's Joe Malone, who had a fourteen-game streak in 1917-18. He had thirty-five goals during his streak.

In third place is Montreal's Newsy Lalonde, with thirteen in 1920-21, and Los Angeles's Charlie Simmer, with thirteen in 1979-80. So I was tied for third, right?

Wrong.

I missed two games with injuries, on January 29 and 31. According to NHL rules for such things, that ended my streak. Figure that one out.

After being horrified in October, at the possiblity of failure, I finished with the third-highest goal total in NHL history. My eighty-six was second only to Gretzky's record ninety-two in 1981-82 and eighty-seven in 1983-84.

But my goal-scoring accomplishments didn't make it any easier for me to accept the Blues' post-season disappointment.

We played excellent hockey in the regular season, particularly in the last forty games. We were 25-10-5 in the second half of the season, and finished with a seven-game winning streak. Back-to-back losses to Chicago in mid-March is probably all that separated us from finishing first overall. The Blues' 105 points were second to the Blackhawks' 106.

That's why our loss to the Minnesota North Stars in the playoffs was so frustrating. Caron says, even though we finished the season with a winning streak, he wondered if "I was going to the Derby with a horse that could be tiring."

"I had it in my mind we might be vulnerable," he said.

But I don't think we were a tired hockey team. We just didn't execute well against the North Stars. Minnesota kept getting the early lead, and we'd have to play catch-up hockey. We weren't playing well enough offensively — particularly on the power play — to make that happen.

Minnesota coach Bob Gainey decided to have Stewart Gavin and Gaetan Duchesne take turns shadowing me. It wasn't the first time any team shadowed, and it probably won't be the last. At least I hope it isn't, because a team would only shadow you if you scored some goals.

The shadowing didn't bother me as much as our inability to take advantage of it. As soon as the shadow appeared, I went right to the net and parked by one of their defenseman. In effect, I created a four-on-four situation and, hopefully, a four-on-three situation, if I could somehow get the defenseman to pay some attention to me.

The North Stars played well defensively, and we didn't jump in the holes.

That surprised me, because we had played so well in advancing to the Norris Division Final. The Detroit Red Wings took a 3-1 lead against us in the best-of-seven series. We came back to win Game Five in St. Louis, then beat the Red Wings in Detroit, to force a seventh game.

In that game, Adam Oates made what I considered his best pass. Typically, *he* says his best pass came in a game against the New York Islanders. But, given the importance, this was his best pass.

It was a tight-checking contest, tied 1-1 late in the second period. I was in the neutral zone, skating toward the bench, when Oatsie got the puck in our zone. When I saw he had the puck, I started to skate across the ice. As if sensing I was there, he blindly backhanded a pass up-ice. He caught me on the fly, and I turned up-ice and went by Detroit defenseman Steve Chiasson. My shot beat goaltender Tim Cheveldae, with twenty-one seconds left in the period, for the go-ahead goal. We won 3-2, and got ready for Minnesota.

We had little time to prepare for the North Stars. Still, there's always time for the crossword. Let's try 14 across. Hmmm. Six-letter word for "man capable of magic." Must be W-I-Z-A-R-D.

Probably, it should be O-A-T-S-I-E.

ST. LOUIS

CHAPTER 12

WILD

OATES

AND

BERRY

The first time I heard about the trade that brought Adam Oates from the Detroit Red Wings to the Blues, I was somewhat miffed.

I was thinking, *How can they trade Bernie Federko?*

Now don't get me wrong. I knew Adam Oates was an excellent player, and that Caron had robbed the Red Wings. But Bernie and Brian Sutter *were* the St. Louis Blues; it didn't seem right for the Blues to trade Bernie. Seeing Federko in a Red Wings uniform was unnatural; it was like hearing Neil Young doing a rap song.

Now, three years later, I can't imagine the Blues without Adam Oates. He's without a doubt the NHL's best passer this side of Wayne Gretzky. There was a period, around the NHL All-Star break, during which Oatsie and I combined for eighty points and the Blues were 12-3. I had twenty-two goals and fourteen assists, and Adam had eight goals and thirty-six assists.

A reporter asked Oatsie if he was satisfied with his recent performance. "You always believe you can do more," he said. "And besides, Brian would shoot me if he heard me say, 'I'm satisfied'"

"Hull and Oates" had become the NHL's hottest act — two artists hitting a high note in perfect harmony. It was uncanny how well we were clicking.

Paul MacLean believes Oatsie, like Gretzky, sees the game at a different speed than the rest of us. The great ones play at a high tempo, while their minds slow down the action so they can see plays developing. Oatsie knows when to snap the pass away to you, when to feather it to you, or when to lead you, like San Francisco 49ers quarterback Joe Montana hitting Jerry Rice on the fly.

"You guys are like Ying and Yang on the ice," Blues trainer Mike Folga said.

Caron has made so many trades since coming to the Blues, in 1983, that there are only a handful of guys on the team who signed their original contracts with the Blues. But the deal for Oatsie was among his best, even if I hated to see Bernie go. The Blues got Oatsie and Paul MacLean for Bernie and Tony McKegney.

It took a long time before we became linemates; but we became instant friends. Oatsie is from Weston, Ontario. He was a lacrosse player when he was younger, and he played that game the way he plays hockey. He was the set-up man for the team's top scorer, Steve Thomas, now a left wing for the Chicago Blackhawks. Oatsie's career has some similarity to mine; he wasn't considered a top NHL prospect, because he wasn't considered a top skater. Scouts changed their minds after watching him perform at RPI.

We aren't all that much alike — which is probably what makes our friendship so interesting. At any given time, he's generally more serious than I am about everything except hockey. He studies every NHL statistic. I barely look at them. I'm outgoing. He's introspective. I'm a goal scorer. He's a passer. It's a perfect relationship.

We live near each other and often ride to the rink together. We room together on the road. Someone asked Adam what we talk about, and he said, "You get a paper, you see an issue, we talk about it."

Oatsie is among the smartest people I know. When he left RPI after his sophomore season, to sign with the Detroit Red Wings, he created his own educational incentive program. His $1.5 million contract is still among the richest ever given to a college free agent. Worried that he wouldn't return to finish his degree, Oatsie had the Red Wings include a clause that punished him if he did not. He gave the team the right to withhold $6,000 of his salary, if he didn't return to college each summer to work on his degree in management. He finished his degree work this past summer.

All of Oatsie's moves, on and off the ice, are calculated. He recently got his first big-time endorsement deal with Pepsi. My soda endorsement deal is with Coke. So what did Oatsie do this summer? He wrote a term paper on the advertising strategy of Coke vs. Pepsi. His conclusion was that competition is good for both sides.

We have been working together on some deals, like the "Hull and Oates" posters and T-shirts. With his talent and model-citizen image, he's likely to draw more and more interest in the marketing world. Those who inquire will find out that Oatsie is extremely choosy about his deals. Count on the fact that he won't ever do anything, just to make money.

"I'm not a clown," he says. "I don't juggle."

Class is what Oatsie is about. When he wanted more money, he had his agent negotiate behind the scenes. No fuss. No public outburst. He hates reading about athletes, like Oakland As outfielder Rickey Henderson, who make their salary negotiations a public ego trip. The difficulty of his climb gives Oatsie a different perspective on the view from the top. He admires athletes who silence critics by performance, rather than with their mouths.

Oatsie enjoyed watching St. Louis Cardinals shortstop Ozzie Smith play well last summer, after everyone had written him off in the off-season. Oatsie is already planning how he can change his game to accommodate getting older.

"I love it when I look at (Baltimore Orioles) Cal Ripken having a great season," Oatsie said. "Everyone was telling him to take a rest, and he stuck it right back at them."

I told Adam once about my first impression of him. He could tell by my grin that I was winding up to zing him.

"I'm remembering back to Minnesota-Duluth when we were about to play you, and everyone is talking like you're this big, strong, great player," I said. "Then I see you. You're just this wimpy guy on skates."

He laughed. He likes to remind me about RPI's triple-overtime win against Minnesota-Duluth in the semifinals. That was the game in which he set an NCAA record of five assists.

"As I recall, I think you missed a breakway in overtime," Oatsie started.

"I didn't. I wouldn't miss on an overtime break-away."

"I'm sure it was you."

"It was not."

"Nope. It was you."

When Coach Mike Sertich came down from Duluth to Bloomington, Minnesota, to watch me play against the Minnesota North Stars, I hauled him over to meet Adam. While we were talking, I called upon Sertich to verify my story.

"No," Sertich said, "Brett didn't miss a breakaway that game."

Oatsie nodded. Then, as soon as Sertie left, he turned to me and said, "I don't care what you or your coach says. You missed the breakaway." OK, Oatsie, one last time, for the record: *I DID NOT MISS A BREAKAWAY IN THE GAME AGAINST RPI!*

Digging on each other is part of our relationship. We get pretty competitive, particularly on the golf course. I give Susie only one rule about my public appearances for the Blues. "Never, never," I said, "cancel golf for any reason."

Golf is a great game. Give me a tee time and I'm there. It's even better when you play for some stakes. Last spring, Oatsie was part of my foursome at Algonquin Country Club near St. Louis. Neither one of us was playing all that well going into the fifteenth hole. We were playing even. Then I suggested: Loser of the next hole buys the dinner. As soon as Adam agreed, I hit a monstrous drive, knocked an iron to the green and drained a thirty-foot birdie putt, with a grin as wide as the St. Louis arch. Oates, who settled for a par, just shook his head.

There was a time, a few years ago, when I would have told you that a left-handed centre would be a must for me. That's one of the time-honored theories of hockey: you want to put a left-handed scorer with a right-handed right winger so the set-up is always feeding the scorer with forehand passes.

The best example of that is left-handed-shooting Wayne Gretzky feeding right-handed Jari Kurri all those years in Edmonton. New York Islanders Bryan Trottier and Mike Bossy were another left-right combo.

But Berry always told me that was overrated. "If you have a good centre, it doesn't matter," Berry said. "Look at a guy like Stan Mikita. He passed just as well on his backhand as his forehand."

My attitude about that changed as soon as I played with right-handed Adam Oates.

Blues Assistant Coach Bob Berry is probably the other guy on the team who understands me as well as Oatsie. Berry is former head coach of Los Angeles, Montreal and Pittsburgh. He appreciates that, as an assistant coach, he can be closer to the players than he could when he was in charge of teams.

"Bob," Oatsie said, "you're just like one of us, only older."

He got the job with the Blues by putting in a 5:30 a.m. phone call to Caron, who once coached Berry in the Canadiens' farm system. Caron says Berry is one of the best all-around athletes he's ever seen. He played well enough as a catcher to get a tryout with the major league baseball team in Houston. They were called the Houston Colt 45s, not the Astros, when Berry tried out.

He had enough talent as a football player to be offered a scholarship to the University of Kentucky. "He played the same position as Rocket Ishmail," Caron told me.

Berry did play for the Quebec Rifles in the Continental Football League, and had an offer to play with the Ottawa Rough Riders of the CFL. He opted instead to sign with the Montreal Canadiens as a left wing.

"When you grew up watching Maurice Richard, Dickie Moore and Jacques Plante in Montreal, they were your idols and legends," Berry said. "Hockey was my first love."

He was sold to Los Angeles in 1970, and played seven seasons there. His best season was in 1972-73, when he scored thirty-six goals.

Our relationship is difficult to explain; all I know is that, when Bob Berry tells me something, I know he's giving it to me straight. When I'm playing poorly, he tells me. When I'm playing well, he tells me. Same tone of voice.

He's the buffer between Brian and the players. "When I was a head coach, I was mostly a jerk," Berry said. "I enjoy being able to pat players on the back now and then, instead of pounding on the desks."

He's always on me about my weight. But somehow, it never bothers me — he comes across like a friend doing you a favor, rather than a coach ordering you to do something.

"If you don't think two or three pounds makes a difference," he says, "then think about how they handicap horse races by two or three pounds."

We have a regular thing going. We'll be at the airport or the rink, and I'll try to get him to tell me who's going to be in the lineup for that night's game. Then, he'll pretend that he's about to reveal some highly-classified piece of information. He'll look around, like he's afraid someone might be looking.

"Don't tell Brian, or I'll get in trouble," he says.

We both start laughing, because the news he provides me is always totally insignificant.

Because I was playing so well with Zezel in 1989-90, Oatsie and I only played together on the power play in his first season in St. Louis. After Zezel was traded, Berry and I talked about whether Oatsie and I would compliment each other.

Berry told me chemistry — not our talent level — would decide whether we were right for each other.

"You need a special player to meld with another top player," Berry said. "It's always said that anyone can play with Wayne Gretzky or Marcel Dionne. That's not true."

Berry remembers the search the Los Angeles Kings went through, trying to find the perfect left wing for Dionne. "They searched and searched — they must have gone through fifteen guys before they came up with Charlie Simmer," Berry said. "In my last year, even I played over there."

He was coaching the Kings when Simmer became the final piece of the Triple Crown line.

"A reporter asked me what my best coaching decision was that season. I said, 'Bringing up Charlie Simmer from the minors.' He said, 'What was your worst decision?' I said, 'Sending Simmer down to the minors after training camp.'"

Before the 1990-91 season, I started to lobby for Oatsie. I probably should have gone right to Brian Sutter; instead I did my talking in the press.

Brian had his reasons for not wanting us together; one theory of hockey is, you try to balance your scoring attack so that your best players aren't all on one line. Certainly, you could make a case for that. We resisted any attempt to say we wouldn't work well together because Oatsie and I both shot right-handed.

"My answer to that," Oatsie said, "is, how many pretty goals do you see scored with that kind of perfect pass? Most goals aren't pretty goals."

Oatsie and I figured the real key to the success of a first line was having a strong second line. One of the reasons Gretzky and Kurri were successful was that they had Mark Messier's line playing right behind them. Having a strong second line took some of the heat off Gretzky and Kurri.

Sudsy did try us together at the start of the season. We were awful. We were trying so hard to stay together, we didn't play our normal game. The team wasn't playing very well. He split us up again. In hindsight, maybe that was good for us, because it showed me that I would still score goals no matter with whom I played. And it certainly increased our desire to be linemates.

We played frequently together on the power play, but had nothing sustained until the All-Star break. With the team struggling offensively, Brian decided to put us together. Oatsie was awesome in the second half of the season; he had three or more assists in twelve of his last thirty-three games. Only four times in the last forty games was the opposition able to hold him pointless.

He finished with 115 points in sixty-one games. Oatsy missed nineteen games, due to injury. When the season was over, he was repeatedly asked if he thought about what kind of season he would have had if he hadn't lost one-fourth of it to injury. Curiously, he thought the injury was one of the advantages he had during the second half of the season. "I think the injury has given me one advantage, in that I'm well-rested right now, when other players aren't," Oates said.

Oatsie and I talk about the game constantly. What I'm about to tell you will be difficult to believe, because I led the NHL, with 389 shots on goal — that's an average of almost five per game. But Oatsie keeps telling me that I give up too many scoring chances, by passing.

At this point, you need both some background and some information about my philosophy on scoring.

Consistency is my trademark; I only like to get a goal or two every game, and let it go at that. I've had forty-three multiple-goal games in my last 158. Last season, I scored at least one goal in fifty-six of seventy-eight games. In the second half of the season, I was only goalless in six of thirty-eight games. For the past two seasons, I have scored at least one goal against every team.

At one stretch, I had at least one goal in thirteen consecutive games, not counting two games I didn't play because of injury.

But I haven't had a four-goal game since my days in Penticton. Despite having goal-scoring seasons of forty-one, seventy-two and eighty-six goals, I only have nine hat tricks. During my eighty-six-goal season, I only had four. I've never had an empty-net NHL goal; I had to work not to get one last season. I had a 'gimme' empty-netter late in the season, but luckily found Tom Tilley free for the pass. He drilled it.

Mostly, I don't like to show up the other team by pouring in goals during a romp. The only time I push extra hard for a third goal is if the game is still on the line. And if I accidently score three goals, I sure don't want a fourth. The only way I'll score four is if the last one is a 'gimme'.

If you are completing hat tricks in a 7-2 rout, then the opposition is going to remember. Next time, they will put much more energy into checks, to prevent you from scoring. I also don't like showboating. Unless a millenium passes between your goals, there's no reason to be throwing yourself on the ice, or getting spastic, just because you scored. Raising your stick is the acceptable signature for a goal scorer. Anything else just shows up the other team.

When I have a chance for a hat trick in a onesided game, and pass the puck, it drives Oatsie nuts. Sometimes, if it's a blowout, I'll even wait for a teammate to catch up, so I'll have someone to pass to.

We'll come back to the bench after I've dished off on a two-on-one break, and Oatsie will roll his eyes like a high school coach admonishing one of his students. "That was the stupidest pass the world has ever seen."

"The world will not think you are a puck hog, if you get three or four goals in a game," Oatsie says. "You are supposed to get goals. You are a goal scorer."

One point Oatsie makes that does make sense, is that playing too relaxed might result in an injury.

"You're in a shooting position and the defense comes after you like you will shoot," Oatsie says.

"Your mindset is *pass*, so you're relaxed. I would hate to see you get hurt because you're being too nice."

That's something to think about. But I don't think I'll ever change. One of the few times I was pressing for goals was last season, during my attempt to get fifty goals in fifty games.

I've always believed that you shouldn't look beyond your next game. I don't like to set goals. But heading toward the All-Star Game in Chicago, there was considerable interest in my chance to become only the fifth player in NHL history to score fifty in fifty. I'd be lying, if I said I didn't start to think about it.

The 50-50 Club is pretty exclusive; Maurice "Rocket" Richard did it first in 1944-45, followed by Mike Bossy in 1980-81, Wayne Gretzky in 1981-82 and then again in 1983-84 and 1984-85, and finally Mario Lemieux in 1988-89.

I scored two goals against the New York Rangers on January 5, and two against New Jersey on January 8, to put me on line with forty-four in forty-three games.

Going into a January 15 game against Washington, I had forty-five goals in forty-five games. I ripped a wrist shot through the pads of Caps goaltender Don Beaupre, thirty-seven seconds into the game, for my forty-sixth. By late in the second period, I had added three more assists, for my second four-point game of the season.

Just before the end of the period, Washington defenseman Joel Quenneville made an innocent dive toward me.

His two hundred pounds went *thud* on my leg. Initially, I thought the All-Star break was in my ankle.

ST. LOUIS

CHAPTER 13

HART
TO
HART

My chances of scoring fifty goals in fifty games were better than fifty-fifty. At least, that's what Oatsie assured me.

The injury wasn't nearly as bad as it seemed, when Quenneville first dropped his load of bricks on me. The diagnosis was a sprain. The weirdest aspect of the injury was that it only hurt when I put on a skate. Walking on it wasn't a problem. But when I attempted to play on it, two days later against Montreal, I was useless. I couldn't make those three quick strides needed to push off. We lost 4-2, and I didn't come close to locating the net.

Fortunately, or unfortunately, depending on your perspective, a break was in the schedule. We were headed into the All-Star weekend. The bad news: I couldn't play in the All-Star Game in Chicago. The good news: four days off allowed my ankle more healing time before I continued my quest for fifty in fifty.

Missing the All-Star Game was extremely disappointing, because it was in the city where Dad had become a legend. It would have been nice to hear the boisterous Chicago Stadium fans cheering for me for a change. I was also the leading vote-getter in fan balloting, with more than 400,000 votes. I felt an obligation to those who voted for me. But we were chasing the Blackhawks for first place in the division, with less than half the season remaining. It wasn't a difficult decision.

The amusing part was that Oatsie replaced me in the All-Star Game, and almost stole the show. He had a goal and four assists; he would have won the car as the game's MVP if he hadn't set up the Toronto Maple Leafs' Vincent Damphousse for three of his All-Star-record four goals. Damphousse was named MVP.

Oatsie should have been invited to the All-Star Game without the help of my ankle. He was bypassed by Campbell Conference coach John Muckler, even though at All-Star time he was second to Wayne Gretzky in points-per-game. When Brian Sutter asked him to replace me, Oatsie wasn't sure he wanted to do it. He suggested Sudsy ask Rick Meagher, who had been the Selke Award winner the previous season, as the league's top defensive player.

"You should have gone last year," Brian said. "But there are years when you deserve to go and don't get invited. And there will be years when your numbers aren't real good and you will get invited. I would like you to go."

"Then, I'm honored," Oatsie said.

Oatsie was on such a roll (fifteen assists in four games) that I should have known I was going to get my fifty in fifty. After getting two in a loss to Minnesota on January 22, I had forty-eight goals in forty-eight games. It would come down to a home-and-home series against the Detroit Red Wings. They had shut me out in three of the five previous meetings that season.

The only time I seem to get nervous is when I'm on course to break some record. The more I think, the worse it gets. It happened the year before, when I was trying to break Kurri's record for goals by a right winger, during the 1989-90 season.

After scoring my seventieth, to tie the record, I was blanked in consecutive games against Los Angeles, Boston and Pittsburgh. I felt as though I was shooting blanks; it seemed like I was getting ten shots per game, yet nothing was going in. The Blues lost six of the last seven games. It wasn't pressure I felt so much as disappointment.

With one regular-season game remaining against the North Stars, Ron Caron sensed I wasn't quite myself. He hadn't ever said much to me about the way I performed. At the morning skate, he called me aside.

"You're not being Brett Hull," he said.

"What do you mean?"

"You're not relaxed. You're pressing. Don't worry so much. You'll get the record. Don't force the play," Caron said. "You aren't having any fun."

"You got that right," I said.

"Then play it your way. You're upset. You're getting down on yourself, which is the price you pay to become great. Do me a favor. Stay in your own zone a little longer, criss-cross to the other side and things will work out. You will be left with one checker. You beat this guy and you will have your scoring chance."

I scored twice that night — the first one coming on a play similar to the one Caron described. I picked up a loose puck, beat Gaetan Duchesne, then whistled a thirty-footer over goaltender Jon Casey's shoulder. It was an amazing relief. I wanted that record. And Caron had sensed the strain of a long season had started to get to me. I had never before played eighty games. I was mentally tired.

Maybe Oatsie sensed I was pressing for fifty. The morning of the first game against Detroit, he brought it up.

"Don't worry. You're going to score tonight," he said. "If we play our game, we know we will get lots of chances. It's as simple as that."

It was that simple. The Red Wings checked me tightly for two periods; I only had a couple of shots on goal. But late in the period, Jeff Brown spotted me alone in the left circle. As Red Wings defenseman Rick Zombo came out to meet me, I ripped a shot past him and goaltender Tim Cheveldae. With one goal in the bag, I started to relax.

Early into the next period, Oatsie set me up for my fiftieth. He picked up the puck ten feet from the blue line and fed me over the stick of a Red Wings player. Shot. Goal. A place in NHL history.

After the goal, Red Wings fans gave me a standing ovation. That's why hockey fans are the best. In another minute, the fans would be screaming for one of their defenseman to nail me. But not at this moment.

To be alongside Richard, Bossy, Gretzky and Lemieux is quite an honor — especially when you consider who *hasn't* done it. Dad did it in the WHA, but not in the NHL. There are great NHL scorers who have never reached that mark. Also amazing to me is that Gretzky scored fifty in thirty-nine games, during 1981-82. That seems impossible to break. I was only the third player to net fifty in less than fifty games. Gretzky scored fifty in forty-two and fifty in forty-nine. Lemieux netted fifty in forty-six, during the 1988-89 season.

The other thing I think about is how many guys have to work together to create the chances for my goals. I'm not a flashy player who creates his own chances; I need someone to get me the puck.

The night I netted my fiftieth, Bob Bassen and Rich Sutter and defenseman Scott Stevens worked like crazy to get the puck out of our zone. No one talked about it. yet clearly everyone worked to help me reach the milestone. We won the game, 9-4.

Another thing I remember is Oatsie becoming hacked off at me, because I wouldn't go for the hat trick. Later in the game, I passed the puck on a couple of good scoring chances.

When we got back to the bench, Oatsie screamed, "SHOOT THE PUCK! SHOOT THE PUCK! FILL YOUR HAT"

I didn't fill my hat. And my season didn't seem to suffer as a result. This milestone sent me on my way to a season of many rewards.

There's one story about my contract that I've been saving. It's one team president Jack Quinn tells better than anyone. He can tell it with a laugh — which is what I like about him.

We were all but finished with the contract, when my agent, Bob Goodenow, decided to go for the cherry to put on the top of the sundae.

"There is one more thing we want," Bob said.

"What is it now?" Quinn said, obviously expecting the worst.

"We want a bonus if Brett wins the Hart Trophy."

"How much?"

"One hundred thousand dollars."

"That's too much money"

"We only want it for one season"

Then Quinn paused for a moment. He told me later that he weighed the proposal logically. He thought about my ability, then considered the NHL still had Gretzky, Lemieux and Steve Yzerman. *What are the odds*, he thought, *that Brett Hull will be the NHL's most valuable player this season?*

"I'll do it," Quinn said.

As it turned out, the odds were pretty good. One year later, I was standing up at the podium, to become the first player, other than Gretzky and Lemieux, to win the Hart Trophy in more than a decade. I received forty-four first-place votes, out of sixty-six ballots.

My Hart came twenty-five years after Dad had won his second of two MVP awards. We are the first father-and-son team to win the award. He won in 1964-65 and 1965-66.

My entire family was in attendance at the awards ceremonies in Toronto. My brother, Bobby Jr., congratulated me on an error-free acceptance speech. The year before, when I won the Lady Byng award, I became somewhat tongue-tied. I said something like, "I want to thank my teammates because, if it wasn't for them, I would be one of them." I have no idea what I was trying to say.

Dad walked around the media room smoking a big cigar, like a proud father announcing the birth of a child.

"There was no big ceremony like this when I won," Dad said. "And I didn't get $100,000. Back then, you got a phone call. 'You won it. Here's your $500.' I probably bought a cow with the money."

There're no ranching genes in my blood. Trust me, I won't be buying any cows. But the award meant a great deal to me. Everyone wants to follow their fathers' footsteps, whether they are doctors, lawyers or hockey players. Dad was one of the best. I wanted to emulate him. Winning put me that much closer to doing that.

Obviously, I owe a great deal to Oatsie. In fact, he deserved consideration for MVP. Despite missing those nineteen games because of injury, he still set a Blues record of ninety assists. Project his points-per-game for a full season, and he would total 158 points. That's Gretzky-like production. He was awesomely awesome.

At one point, Brian Sutter was asked whether he thought Oatsie or I should win the MVP. He said, "That's like asking a father which son he likes best."

The other nice aspect of winning the award was that I received it on the same night Sudsy won the Jack Adams Award as coach of the year.

It was the culmination of what had been an unbelievable personal season — beyond anything I could have ever dreamed possible. Only winning the Stanley Cup could have made it better.

Reporters again prodded me to compare myself to Lemieux or Gretzky, which I won't do, because I don't come close to matching their overall skill. They are playmakers, penalty-killers and goal scorers. I'm a goal scorer.

"They also have a Stanley Cup," I said. "Maybe if I get one of those..."

The Stanley Cup is the ultimate. Everything else is secondary. Someone asked me, after I netted fifty in fifty, whether there would be any ribbing of Dad, because I accomplished it in the NHL and he didn't.

"Not a chance," I said. "Because all he has to say is, 'How many Stanley Cups have you won?'"

An NHL player should always be willing to trade any personal honor for a Cup; if you wouldn't do that, then you don't have a clue what the game is all about.

After Caron had suggested I had the potential to score a hundred goals, he told me that he hoped I didn't perceive that as putting all the pressure on me. He said the pressure was on him.

"In order for you to get into that position, we have to get you a better team," Caron said. "And guess what? I'm going to try to do that."

He has done that. And he continues to do that every day. He's the kind of guy who's doing player evaluations three hours before you get out of bed.

The Blues are a class organization. They take care of their players. Oatsie had a contract through 1993-94. His base salary was only $240,000 — which is way out of line in the ever-changing NHL marketplace. They could have fought him, when Oatsie's agent asked about an extension. They didn't. They worked out a deal that added one year and raised his total package by $2 million.

When you win the Hart Trophy, you aren't thinking about the bonus money you will earn. But a few weeks later, it hit me: what a truly excellent contract Bob had negotiated for me, in terms of bonus clauses. When the final tally was complete, I made $723,758.45 in bonus money for the 1990-91 season. The forty-five cents was probably payment for my dressing-room singing. I'm an awesome singer. Just ask my teammates.

One final note about the Hart Trophy ceremony in Toronto. After years of uneasiness between Mom and Dad, there was at least a truce for this event. They are still at odds on too many issues for any permanent friendship. But they finally had an exchange of words that wasn't heated.

After I had won the Hart Trophy, Mom went up to Dad and said, "Congratulations. It's quite a feat to have a father and a son who have both scored fifty goals and both won the Hart Trophy."

Dad thanked her. A few moments later, he approached her. "Congratulations on having an award-winning son."

Brett in action with the St. Louis Blues against the Toronto Maple Leafs. *(Canada Wide)*

Brett receives congratulations from his St. Louis teammates (including Adam Oates, right) in February 1990
after scoring his 59th goal – and topping his father's season high. *(Shaney Komulainen/Canapress)*

Brett with father Bobby in the St. Louis dressing room.
Earlier, Brett scored his fiftieth goal of the 1989-90
season, making Brett and Bobby Hull the only father-
son combination to reach that milestone. *(Darrell
Sandler/Canapress)*

Brett skates with Team U.S.A.: "My decision was about loyalty, not nationalism or patriotism." *(Craig Robertson/Canada Wide)*

St. Louis Blues' coach Brian "Sudsy" Sutter shows off
the Jack Adams Award for NHL coach of the year June
1991. One year later he was fired. Said Brett: "Sudsy
never talked to me about scoring goals. Yet he had his
way of motivating me." *(John Felstead/Canapress)*

Brett signing autographs: "It's great fun being in the limelight and meeting celebrities."

Brett Hull holds the Hart Memorial Trophy at the 1991 NHL Awards Banquet after being named the league's most valuable player. *(Hans Deryk/Canapress)*

ST. LOUIS

CHAPTER 14

ONE
HULLUVA
FAMILY

My brother, Blake, threatens to have a special T-shirt made, to wear at all Hull family functions.

"On the front it will say, 'I used to be Bobby Hull's son,'" he says, "and on the back it will say, 'Now, I'm Brett Hull's brother.'"

Maintaining a sense of humor is crucial to survival in my family. The Hull name can be both a curse and a blessing at the same time; it opens some doors and slams others in your face. My surname comes with a yard-stick by which I will be measured my entire life. It's not that I didn't expect it.

That's the way it always is, when you are the son or daughter of a famous athlete. If Joe Montana has a son, and he doesn't expect to be measured against his father, then he is in serious trouble.

My Uncle Dennis, now a hockey television analyst for the NHL expansion San Jose Sharks, was the first Hull to be compared to Dad. He had the fortune (or is it misfortune?) to play with him on the same NHL team in Chicago.

"Even when I was an All-Star, I was still Bobby Hull's brother," Dennis told a reporter. "No matter what I did, I was going to be Bobby Hull's brother. There was nothing I could do about it, and there was nothing he could do about it."

Dennis said the only way to deal with the situation was to accept it as something he couldn't change.

"You couldn't exactly go up to Bobby and say, 'That was awful rotten of you, to be a superstar and go out and spoil it for the rest of your family.'"

My brothers and I could identify with our uncle's difficulty playing in the same city with Dad. It wasn't easy playing youth hockey in Canada, when your father was the best left wing ever to play in the National Hockey League. When Mom and Dad decided to divorce, there was even more attention on us. The media pulled out the microscopes and magnifying glasses, to make sure they didn't miss even the most trivial bits of information. Mom didn't fill me in on every detail. She didn't have to. I could pick up a newspaper and get plenty of information. Some of it was shocking — but none of the children were surprised that Mom and Dad divorced. The question wasn't "If they get a divorce?" It was more "When will they get a divorce?"

I remember once playing midget hockey in Vancouver during the height of the publicity surrounding the divorce, and someone yelled out from the stands, "Hey, Hull, have you seen your dad lately?"

I didn't even look up, just skated back to the bench, sat down and started joking around with the guys.

"Brett, doesn't that bother you?" someone asked.

"Not at all," I said. "What should I do? Try to beat up everyone who says anything about me, or my family? Actually, I could care less what people think or say about me. And if you react, you give them exactly what they want."

That's always been my attitude. Kids can be cruel. Someone always had something to say to my brothers and me about being a Hull. The only response they ever got from me was a smile. Twenty years later, nothing has changed. Insults are hurled from the stands without ever getting an acknowledgement from me.

There's one that just cracks me up. Once a game, someone will yell at me, "You're about as good as your old man."

And I'm thinking, *Well, thanks. My dad scored more than six hundred goals in the NHL. That's a compliment, you moron. If you want to insult me, you're supposed to say something bad about me. Tell me that I have bad taste in music, if you really want to insult me.*

But, divorce and all, I actually had a blast growing up. My family is now separated by many miles — Bobby Jr. runs a clothing manufacturing shop in Toronto. Blake works for the NHL's Lightning in Tampa, Florida. Bart spent the last summer in the Ottawa Rough Riders training room, rehabilitating a blown knee. Michelle is in pre-med at Western Washington University. There's a possibility she may live with me in St. Louis, and attend nearby Washington University medical school.

Despite the miles separating us, there is no distance between the Hulls. When we are together, it's like we have never been apart. Mom is the glue holding us all together; she's the one who calls me with the family news. Mom, in case you haven't caught on, has an awesome sense of humor. If I'm not calling home often enough, there's always a short message on my answering machine: "Brett, this is your M-O-T-H-E-R, and you won't have one who claims you unless you call me real soon."

Mom deserves some credit for my success. She was supportive, after others had lost faith. Whenever I tried to quit, she wouldn't let me. She pushed me all the way to Penticton. That was probably the most significant five-hour drive I ever took. Mom and I battled at times, but I never doubted she was on my side. I didn't listen to her enough. I'll always be thankful that she had enough trust in me to let me do things on my own.

She was my coach in life. I might not be where I am today if she had allowed me to become an arrogant kid, unable to take criticism. She taught me to accept instruction and keep a good attitude. She allowed me to find out who I was.

And my step-father, Harry, is also a class act. After Mom and Dad divorced, he replaced a Hall of Fame father, and he did an awesome job. He let Mom handle the discipline. He was always there when we needed him. Mom and Harry literally moved mountains to attend almost all of our sporting events. When I played in Penticton, Mom and Harry attended most of my games. It usually took them five hours, traveling down the rugged Princeton Highway.

One time, the snow was so bad that Harry had to find an alternate route and it took him more than eight hours to get to Penticton.

"Harry," I said, "it's just a hockey game. Why even go through all that bother?"

"Because we promised you we would be there," Harry said.

Harry is proud of our accomplishments; he has always treated us as his own kids, not as step-children. Harry and Mom also attended all of Bart's football games at Boise State University. Even now, Mom and Harry watch all of my games on the satellite dish.

Earlier this summer, Mom opened one of the cupboards at home and discovered several ring binders, filled with hockey cards. She opened one and found it filled with Brett Hull hockey cards.

"Oh, it's just a couple of cards I picked up," Harry said.

Michelle loves teasing him about his new hobby. Every time she accuses him of becoming obsessive about collecting, he says he wouldn't even consider himself a collector.

"Harry, you have two thousand cards. What do you mean, you aren't a collector?" she said. Maybe it's Harry's hoarding of Hulls that's driving up the price of my rookie card.

Credit Bobby Jr. and Blake for helping me get to the NHL. First, they played before me, and by the time it was my turn, the novelty of watching Bobby Hull's kid had worn away. Essentially, they made it easier for me, by clearing the path. I made it easier still by never letting the pressure or abuse get to me.

Bobby Jr. says now he let too many things bother him when he played. If hard work by itself would get you to the NHL, Bobby Jr. would be a star. He worked harder than many players who made it to the NHL; he certainly worked harder than I did, growing up.

The weight of the Hull surname was heaviest on Bobby Jr., because he came first. Carrying my dad's first name was not an added bonus, either. No matter how well Bobby Jr. played, his performance failed to measure up. He could score three goals, and people in the stands were always yapping at him. "Hull, you're a disgrace to your name," someone would yell. Or, "You'll never be half the player your father was."

When Bobby Jr. played Junior A hockey, opposing players went after him — as if taking a run at the son of a Hall of Famer was some sort of honor.

"My problem," Bobby Jr. says now, "was I always took everything way too seriously. When someone said something, I let it bug me. Then I would want to prove something to everyone, and I'd get too nervous to play."

Bobby Jr. also felt like he was caught up in Dad's hockey politics. In the mid-'70s, Dad began to speak out publicly about unnecessary violence in the game. This was the heyday of goonism. It was the period of Broad Street Bullies dominating the NHL. No one ever bothered Dad in the WHA, because they knew better; they would have found themselves chewing on Dad's stick. His Winnipeg Jets teammates, Ulf Nilsson and Anders Hedberg, were getting brutalized every game. Some Canadian players resented Europeans migrating to the NHL and WHA, because they viewed it as foreigners stealing jobs from Canadians. Nilsson and Hedberg didn't fight back, so they were immediately labeled "Chicken Swedes."

Dad watched Anders and Ulfie take one too many high sticks. He decided he'd had enough. He sat out a Jets' game in protest — hoping the hockey community would take notice and make some changes. It didn't happen.

Bobby Jr., meanwhile, was playing for Lethbridge in the Western Junior Hockey League. The team had a reputation for tough play. When Dad went to a practice and saw kids bringing in boxing gloves, he wasn't happy. Bobby Jr. said the gloves were only used for hitting punching bags after practice, but Dad said he wanted him to leave. He didn't like that kind of hockey.

"I don't want to leave," Bobby Jr. said. "They aren't making me fight."

Dad said he was concerned about Bobby Jr.'s safety.

"There are only twenty games left; let me stay the rest of the season," Bobby said.

"Don't make me force you to leave," Dad said.

Bobby Jr. came home, and didn't play the rest of the season. The following season, some teams from the Ontario Hockey League called about Bobby Jr., and Dad told them, "You will have to pay him more money than you pay your usual players."

Dad, underpaid early in his career, was trying to get the best deal for his oldest son. Bobby Jr. didn't see it that way. "I don't want more money. I just want to play a regular shift," he said.

He picked Cornwall, Ontario, because it was close to where my dad was going to live, in Belleville.

Bobby Jr. called Cornwall General Manager Gordie Wood and told him he didn't want extra money. "Just assure me that I'm going to play regularly," he asked.

Wood assured him he would. He even promised Bobby Jr. would be in the power play. It never quite worked out that way.

The Cornwall coach was Doug Carpenter, who later went on to coach in the NHL. On the first day of camp, Bobby Jr. had just completed the five-mile fitness run as a reporter came up to him. "I just talked to Carpenter and asked about your arrival. Carpenter said, 'I didn't want him.'"

He played on a line with future NHLers Dale Hawerchuk and Scott Arniel. He had a great training camp. But when the season began, he was on the bench. He kept asking to be traded, and Wood kept insisting they had plans for him if he remained patient. The whole season went that way.

The following season was more of the same. He did get a tryout with the Toronto Maple Leafs. He never made it.

Dad always says Bobby Jr.'s only problem was that he never ended up on the right team. Dad also recognizes that he had inadvertently made it more difficult for his oldest son to succeed in a sport he loved.

"If I knew I was going to score so many goals in the National Hockey League," Dad says now, "I never would have given him my full name."

Blake played Tier II hockey for the Dixie Bee Hives in Mississauga, Ontario, and also tried to play at Cornwall. He had more skills than I had; he could skate and shoot better. Neither one of us spent every minute thinking about hockey; we liked to have a great time off the ice. I got the breaks on the ice. He didn't.

Our philosophy on hockey was the same; we both believed that most players approached the game wrong. Everyone seemed to want to make the game complicated, and we wanted to simplify it.

"You don't play hockey to crash and bang," Blake said. "You play to create scoring opportunities."

I couldn't have said it better myself.

Blake swears he never really considered himself an NHL prospect. He said he played the game because it was fun, not because it was a career aspiration. "It gave me something to do in the winter — that's all," Blake says.

Blake and I had some great times together in North Vancouver. He would come home in the summer, and we would hang out together. We played a lot of sandlot sports. We were an awesome passing combination. We'd diagram plays for everyone and, when the huddle was breaking up, I would turn to him and say simply, "Go long." He'd just nod.

Completely ignoring the play we drew up, he would bust downfield and I would spiral a sixty-yarder. Blake would run under it and snare the ball in full gallop. It worked every time.

Blake has another talent; he is an excellent golfer. He became an assistant professional at La Gorce

Country Club in Miami Beach, and also tried the PGA mini-tour in Florida for a year. Blake, whose best round is a sixty-six, finished sixth in one event at four under par, but struggled the rest of the season, with good cause.

A back injury made it difficult to walk, let alone play golf. The pain was so severe at times that he would actually have to roll out of the bed each morning, to get to the floor. He would pop some Advils and a prescribed muscle relaxant, and stay there until the pain subsided enough to allow him to get up.

"It's strange," Blake said. "I played hockey with three broken bones in my hand, and Dad played a couple of times with a broken jaw. But golf is the one sport you can't play if you just aren't right."

Bart was probably the smartest, because he pursued football instead of hockey. He is the best all-around athlete in the family. At age ten, he had a neck fusion to repair damage done by a fall at school. That didn't slow him down. He could dunk a basketball before he grew to six feet. He ran track and built himself a physique that puts me to shame. In fact, he was so muscular when he arrived at Boise State to play football that he was plagued repeatedly by pulled muscles. Coaches told him if he didn't improve his flexibility, then he was never going to be able to last an entire season.

Bart only carried the ball about a hundred times during his three-season career at Boise State. Those had to be among the most effective hundred carries in the school's history. His teammates called him "Touchdown Bart."

Despite nagging injuries, he played backup tailback and fullback. He played behind Chris Thomas, a sure bet to finish second on the school's all-time leading rusher list.

But Bart was Number One at locating the end zone. He carried the ball sixty-five times in his junior season, for 253 yards and seven touchdowns. Before that, he had carried the ball thirty-five times, for seventy-eight yards and four touchdowns. His best performance came during the only football game Dad ever saw him play. Dad flew down to watch a home game against the University of Nevada-Reno, which was ranked second in the U.S.A. for Division 1 AA schools.

Bart carried the ball three times during the game, and scored three touchdowns on runs of one, eight and one yard.

The British Columbia Lions made Bart a first-round pick in the Canadian Football League draft, after this junior year.

When I see him now, I can't believe it's the same kid I used to dominate in basketball. I remember when he learned to play basketball. He regularly wanted to play against me, because he figured it was one game I didn't know. He was right. But after playing for a few weeks, I was able to can twenty-foot jumpers. It drove him crazy.

First and foremost, Bart will always be my little brother. That means he must put up with a fair amount of grief coming his way. I remember this summer, he was telling me about the contract problems he was having with the B.C. Lions of the CFL. They were offering him about $2,500 to sign, and $30,000 for his first season.

"Heck, I'll give you that just for taking the tree stumps out of my backyard in Duluth," I told him.

The youngest child in my family is Michelle. Her experiences in the Hull family are quite different than the boys'. She could probably write a book with some interesting anecdotes from her perspective. Michelle will have to put up with being my kid sister forever. She's engaged to be married and planning to be an orthopedic surgeon, and I'm still introducing her as "my little sister."

One thing I remember, growing up with her, was that she had some pluck. When she was about eleven, she would always try to sing along with the radio. I would always stop her in mid-note.

"Do you know all of the words to this song?" I would ask.

"Not all of them."

"Then you can't sing. You're only allowed to sing in my presence if you know all the words."

This routine went on for months. She'd try to sing; I'd cut her off.

One day, The Steve Miller Band's rendition of "Take the Money and Run" came on. She started singing. I started to cut her off.

"I know every word, and I'm going to sing this song!" she asserted.

And she did, louder and prouder than Steve Miller ever has or ever will. Michelle has spunk, which is another Hull characteristic. Michelle took plenty of teasing from all of her older brothers. One thing I remember doing was telling her I was going to put the family cat in the trash compactor. She tells me now that those days are going to come back to haunt me.

Here's how she's got the scenario figured out: it's late in my career, and my knee is blown out. I need her surgical skills to give me a few more years in the NHL. I'm lying strapped to the table. My knee is split open; all of the cartilage exposed. She's standing over me with a scalpel in hand. As she leans over to me, she whispers, "Before we start, I just want to say six words to you. Remember the cat and trash compactor!"

Ouch!

The wildest weekend a family ever had in Winnipeg might have occurred in June of 1990, when the Hull clan rolled in for Bobby Jr.'s wedding.

It was the first time the four boys and Michelle had been together in one place in about ten years. We were so happy to see each other that we were all acting goofy. When one brother went to the bathroom, the other three followed in unison. It was like we didn't want to be separated.

Mom and Harry were with us on our first stop, and we ran up about a $230 tab. Just for old times' sake we stuck Harry with the bill. Of course, I promised to pay him back. That's only about a billion dollars I owe him now.

We moved next to Grapes' Pier Seven. We really let loose. Mardi, Bobby Jr.'s fiancée, didn't drink, so she was entrusted to get us all home. If you are going to celebrate, you have to act responsibly. We all know there are times you shouldn't get behind the wheel of a car. In her role as designated driver, she had a chance to see the Hull clan at our best and our worst at the same time.

What a crazy night. The room was packed. We put on an enthusiastic exhibition of singing and dancing. The only thing uglier than three Hull boys gyrating on the dance floor is four Hull boys gyrating on the dance floor. At one time, three-quarters of the people crowded into the bathroom to watch Bart demonstrate how he could remove a stall door in a millisecond, with a forearm shiver.

Next, Blake convinced Bart he should be more protective of our sister. So, when a guy came over to talk to Michelle, he was greeted by a six-foot, 215-pound fullback, who said simply, "You touch my sister, you die."

Of course, when the poor guy left, all of us, including Michelle, laughed like crazy.

None of us wanted the night to end. As it drew to a close, Blake gathered most of the crowd around the instant breathalyzer machine. This machine is important enough that they should probably be available in the United States, too. They measure the alcohol content in blood, and let you know if you should drive. Of course, we knew we had too much, but we wanted to test anyway.

Bobby Jr. stepped up first and blew into the straw. The red light went on—too intoxicated to drive. Everyone cheered. And the Hulls banded together, arms locked as if they were about to huddle up.

Blake went next, and the result was the same. More cheering. More Hull huddling. More revelry.

I was next, and the place erupted again when the red light came on. More huddling. More cheering. By then, the place was in a frenzy.

Finally, it was Bart's turn. The little brother who we all used to tease now strode to the machine as the toughest man in the place. He blew into the straw. The green light came on: OK to drive.

A chorus of boos echoed from the crowd. "You've been lagging behind," they jeered.

Bart was inconsolable. Finally, Blake pulled him over and ordered him one straight up. After Bart poured it down, Blake climbed on a chair and announced that Bart was going to "try it again."

Bart blew into the straw. The light turned red. It read "Too intoxicated to drive." The crowd cheered, and the Hull boys lifted little brother on their shoulders and carried him around the room.

We were closer at that moment than we had been since the days in Winnipeg when we played the best games of hockey any group of kids ever played.

ST. LOUIS

Chapter 15

Father
and
Son

My relationship with Dad isn't Ward
Cleaver and the Beaver. It also was
never as strained as portrayed by the
media.

Everyone wants to write the story
about how Dad and I are "renewing"
our relationship, after years of not seeing each other. Our relationship didn't
end; it was just put on hold by circum-
stances. Our story isn't about the re-
conciliation of father and son. Our story
is the unfortunate, all-too-common, tale
about how divorce breaks up a family.
It was distance and circumstance that
kept Dad and me apart — nothing more

and nothing less. The lack of communication between us wasn't about Dad and me. It was about Mom and him. I lived with Mom in Vancouver and he was in Winnipeg, then Chicago. We weren't exactly next-door-neighbors.

Divorce, by its nature, undermines relationships. When one parent isn't even in the same time zone, it makes contact even more difficult. I'm not the only guy who had infrequent contact with a parent, after a divorce. I saw my friends' parents get divorced, and it was always the kids caught in the middle. Where do your Mom and Dad live? If it isn't in the same province or state, how often do you see them? Probably not as much as you should. That's the way it was with my father and me. And neither my dad, nor I, has ever been very accessible by phone. Still, to this day, I really have no idea how to get in touch with him, without a painstaking search. He is always traveling somewhere.

I have great memories of Dad, during his days with the Winnipeg Jets. He wasn't one to get on the ice and teach his kids the game. His idea of teaching was telling us to watch him. We don't play the same style; yet I know that, subconsciously, I learned to become a goal scorer by watching him fly up the ice in Winnipeg. He was like a panther; power and grace harmonized in one perfectly proportioned body. He was beautiful to watch and dangerous to defend against.

It was fascinating to watch him glide up left wing and snap the puck in one fluid motion.

Many NHL players can match, or better, my shot velocity. But twenty-five years ago, Dad's cannon was without peer.

Blues Assistant Coach Bob Berry remembers one occasion when a Hall of Fame goaltender admitted he really didn't want to face Dad's blast. In 1968-69, Berry was called up by the Montreal Canadiens, from their minor league team in Cleveland. Because Berry didn't get many shifts, he took a seat on the bench next to Gump Worsley. He was the backup goaltender to Tony Esposito, for a game against the Blackhawks.

"Esposito either got hurt or was winded," Berry told me. "I remember Gump saying to me, 'I hope he gets up. I don't want to go in there, with Bobby Hull shooting the puck the way he is.' And Gump was very serious."

In 1968-69, there was reason to be more worried about Dad's shooting.

Last season, I led the NHL with 389 shots on goal in 78 games — that was 63 more than anyone else in the league. In 1968-69, Dad had 414 shots on goal in 74 games, to set his personal mark of 58 goals in a season. The only player to have more shots on goal in one season is Phil Esposito, who had 426 in 1971-72 and the amazing league record of 550 in 1970-71.

Even when he was in his late thirties, Dad could dominate. We marveled at the way he would trail the play and wait for opposing defensemen to come to a stop, before ripping into the zone at full tilt. The only similarity in our style is that I also like to head toward our zone during a breakout, then double back to rejoin the play. It's like taking yourself out of the play, to get back in it.

Near the end of Dad's career, he came to Vancouver for a game. My friend, Kelly Muir, and I went to watch him play. After the game, we were in the dressing room talking, while Dad was peeling off his sweater and pads.

Kelly first looked at his barrel chest and anvil-hard arms, and then back at my flabby girth.

"Your old man's forty years old, and he's in better shape than you," Kelly joked. "Look at him — he's an Adonis."

Dad does have a physique like a Greek god. Years of bailing hay, on a farm in southern Ontario, created forearms as thick as tree trunks. He looks like Popeye; his forearms dwarf his biceps. Even at age fifty-two, he's a better physical specimen than many half his age.

One of my favorite moments came in 1986, when I skated on a line with Dad in a Minnesota-Duluth reunion game, in front of 5,600 fans at Duluth Arena. It was a great night, because it also marked the return of Matt Christensen. He played in front of the Bulldog fans for the first time since suffering a near-fatal stroke six months earlier. The fans gave Matt a standing ovation of more than a minute.

Early into the game, I scored what I considered to be a pretty meaningless goal. But Dad didn't quite see it that way. He says, when he watched me play as an eleven-year-old, he always thought I had a chance to be an NHL player. Still, he always believed the only sure way to evaluate a prospect was to play on a line with him.

After I scored, he was grinning. He told me, "As soon as I was skating with you, I knew you could play with anyone, any place, at any time. I knew then you were an NHL player."

Even during the pre-divorce days in Winnipeg, it was difficult for Dad to watch me play, because he would be mobbed. He would sign every autograph and miss most of the game.

When it was over, it would be the typical scene of a dad trying to motivate his son to be a better player.

Mom would say, "You were great, Brett. You scored four goals."

Dad would say, "If you worked a little harder you would have scored five goals."

We laugh about the many times he tried to tell me how to play the game, and I wouldn't listen. As I've said before, we're both rather stubborn about our approach to hockey.

When I was eleven, playing for a Pee Wee team in Winnipeg (future NHLer Richard Kromm was my teammate), Dad came to watch me play. On the way home, he lectured me about how I needed to spend more time in the corners, and less time near the blue line.

"You need to go in there and help your linemates," Dad said.

"My coach tells me to play up high, near the blue line."

"Your coach is an annuity salesman. He has never played the game and never earned a dollar from it. I've been making a living at it for more than twenty years. Who are you going to believe?"

"My coach," I said.

Even though Dad was an NHL star, he had the same parenting style as most fathers in North America. He let Mom handle the discipline — if it was okay with Mom, it was okay with him. And of course he was a player, so he spent half of his time on the road. But we knew how far we could push; if he raised his voice even one decibel we knew it was trouble.

We were always causing a stir. I have never had a hockey fight, but I did try to punch out Blake once, when I was nine and he was eleven. On a long car ride, he did everything in his power to provoke me. He was needling me, poking me and trying everything to get under my skin.

He did a good job. When we got out of the car, I drilled him hard on the nose with a right hand. He was dazed, but I just stood there. Dad was yelling, but as usual, I wasn't paying attention. Blake finally got his wits about him and began to counter-attack.

"Blake, that's enough," was all my dad had to say to bring about a truce.

Dad pulled me up. I figured I was in trouble for starting it. "Next time you have him dazed like that," he said, with a wink, "hammer him again."

Of course, Dad also told us those same stories that all dads tell their kids, about how tough life was when they grew up. Dad's favorite tale involved playing pond hockey.

"You kids have it easy, because there's always a roof over your heads when you play," Dad would say.

"To have clear ice, I shoveled enough snow to cover half of Winnipeg."

We always laughed, because he also told us he baled enough hay to cover the other half of Winnipeg.

But Dad insisted hockey was better in the open air. One night, he decided to prove it to us. He invited Ulf Nilsson, loaded his sons into the car, and drove to the outdoor rink at the community centre. It was already dark when we arrived; the lights weren't on. But Dad spotted some removable boards at the end of the rink. He pulled them off, then drove his car up to the opening he created. His headlights illuminated the rink boards-to-boards. We had an awesome two hours of hockey. Maybe hockey is better on an outdoor rink.

Mostly, I take Bobby Hull's stature for granted, because he's my dad. But he still has impact on other players. During the playoffs in 1990-91, Dad flew into St. Louis to watch Game Five of the opening round against Detroit. We trailed 3-1 in the best-of-seven series. Dad told me he was going into the room before the game, and pump up the guys. "It never hurts to have a new voice," he said.

To me it wasn't a big deal, because he's my dad. He's always trying to tell me how to play. He's my dad. That's his job. I'm the son. I don't listen. That's my job. But then I realized my teammates saw the situation differently. Dad had played for a Stanley Cup championship team, won the NHL scoring title and the league MVP award. He was a Hall of Famer. They liked hearing what he had to say.

"Today's players don't always relate very well to players from my era," Berry told me. "But there are two players they all know — Bobby Orr and Bobby Hull. They all want to know them."

Before the game, he wandered around revving everyone up on a one-on-one basis. He would talk to Vincent Riendeau about stopping Steve Yzerman, and to the defensemen about playing strong along the boards.

"You're big enough to chase bears with a stick," he told Scott Stevens. "Make sure you nail someone tonight."

He'd remind you that you never really know how close you'll get to a Stanley Cup, so you always have to give each playoff bid your best shot.

"I don't think you guys realize how close you are to being a Stanley Cup team," he would say. "This might be the best chance you will have. Don't let it get away from you."

He even predicted the Minnesota North Stars would knock off Chicago in the first round of the Norris Division final.

We won in St. Louis, to make the series 3-2, then Dad came to Detroit and repeated his pre-game pep talks. We won the game to tie the series. He came back to St. Louis and we became the eighth team to rally from a 3-1 deficit, to win an NHL playoff series.

"Next year," Susie Mathieu told him, "we'll bring you in right from the beginning."

I do remember the night he came to see me play against Harvard in the NCAA playoffs. He hadn't seen me play in seven or eight years — since the days in Winnipeg. I was nervous. Here's my dad, the world's greatest left winger, coming to watch me play. The only thing I remember was that I set up the game-winning goal by Norm Maciver.

Of course Dad didn't see much of the game, because he was busy signing a million autographs. A long story about him appeared the next day in the newspaper. He told the reporter that, after hockey season was over, Minnesota-Duluth should recruit me to play baseball. "Brett can hit the ball from here to the lake," he said.

Dad also credited his own success to the work ethic he developed on the farm. "I think I threw around enough bales of hay to cover Duluth," Dad said.

Dad is trying to cover all of North America with that hay he pitched.

We went out to dinner after the game, and I don't remember what we talked about. I think we agreed there would be more more opportunities to see each other when I turned professional. He told me he was proud of me. We talked about playing in the NHL. Dad remembers one other item on the agenda. "I think I tried to say you were playing the game all wrong," Dad says with a laugh, "and you told me you were playing it the way the coach, Mike Sertich, wanted you to play it."

Dad's impact on the game went beyond his on-ice accomplishments. During my contract negotiations with the Blues, Goodenow and I talked regularly about how the league was at the crossroads of salary escalation. Players were raising serious questions about the NHL pay scale. It occurred to me that Dad was raising those questions almost twenty years before. He was way ahead of his time on and off the ice. When he played, he was always crusading for better pay for players. In 1968, he "retired" for three days, until the Blackhawks made him the first NHL player to make $100,000. Now he's still battling for a better deal for retired players. At the All-Star Game in Chicago, he joined several former players in expressing disatisfaction with the NHL's handling of the pension fund.

Dad was a maverick in 1972, when he signed the ten-year deal with the Jets for $2.7 million.

"That was big news back then," Berry said. "That was more than the gross national product of some countries."

A few weeks earlier, Dad had turned down a $1 million, five-year offer from the Blackhawks, before bolting to the rival World Hockey Association. NHL folks were so mad that he wasn't invited to compete in the Summit Series against the Soviets. He still blames Alan Eagleson, Chicago Blackhawks owner Bill Wirtz and late NHL President Clarence Campbell for keeping him off the team.

While some were snubbing him, others were thanking Dad for helping create a new market for players and coaches. During last summer's Canada Cup, former NHL coach Jacques Demers, who was a television commentator, said Dad was responsible for getting him into professional hockey.

The Chicago Cougars of the World Hockey Association approached Demers about becoming director of player development. He was told he would only be hired if Bobby Hull signed with Winnipeg. Everyone was looking for some indication that the rebel league was going to float.

"He gave the WHA legitimacy," Demers said. "And the WHA had jobs for someone like me."

The Cougars hired Demers right after Dad went to Winnipeg. From there he went to the Quebec Nordiques, then the St. Louis Blues and finally the Detroit Red Wings.

"If your dad would have stayed in Chicago," Demers said, "I might not ever have gotten out of Montreal [where he was coaching a junior team]. Not many NHL teams were hiring French Canadians."

Chicago Blackhawks Hall of Famer Stan Mikita said during the 1970s that he always faced west and bowed to Dad in Winnipeg, before he went to bed. Mikita said that, after Dad defected to a rival league, the Blackhawks tripled his salary.

Mikita's ideas about the pay for former players are cloaked in a good sense of humor. When Mikita was scheduled to play in an oldtimers' game in Chicago at the All-Star festivities, SportsChannel asked him to fill out a questionnaire.

The first question: What did you like best about playing in the NHL?

"The paycheque."

What did you like least about the NHL?

"The size of the paycheque."

What has been the most dramatic change in the NHL since you left?

"The paycheques are bigger."

Dad says the most satisfying "Thank you" he ever received came from former NHL player Wayne Cashman, now an assistant coach for the New York Rangers. It was September 1972. Dad was in Vancouver doing promotional work, when he ran into some players who were trying out for Team Canada. He went out with Tony Esposito and Cashman and had drinks.

Dad decided to ask Cashman if he had four spare tickets, so his friend could take his family to the game.

Cashman reached into his pocket and handed him four. According to Dad, the conversation went like this:

"What do I owe you?" Dad asked.

"It's not what you owe me. It's what I owe you," Cashman said. "If it wasn't for you, I would still be making $20,000, instead of $60,000."

Dad has never stopped championing the cause of better pay for players. He still burns about the early days in the NHL, when you had to accept what the teams would pay, or they wouldn't keep you around. Even when I was going after my first NHL contract, Dad pressed me to break the bank. "Go for what you think you're worth," Dad said, "not what the league says you're worth."

Even after Brian Burke convinced Cliff Fletcher to give me a lucrative one-way deal, Dad wasn't satisfied. Even at that time, he thought I should have pushed for more.

When I was negotiating with the Blues, he said right from the beginning that I was a $1 million player. Early in the season, when I was thinking I would settle for around $300,000, he was growling that it was too low.

"You should try the free agency," Dad said. "Go to Detroit, or Los Angeles, where they'll pay you what you're worth."

As you can see, Dad and I don't share the same personality gene that spurs maverick behavior. My personality is more like my mother's than my father's. He enjoys rocking the boat, and I like to steer the course most of the time. Even though I pushed the Blues hard for more money, I always felt a sense of loyalty to them for launching my career. I never would have moved down the road for a few dollars more. However, a million or so would have been a different story.

The Blues gave me a great contract. Dad was happy for me. "But I still think you left a lot more money on the table by not trying free agency," he insisted.

He likes to get in the last word. When Dad shows up in the dressing room, Momesso or Chaser will yell, "Hey, Hullie, your coach is here."

Early last season in Toronto, Dad took the cue. He immediately started to eyeball my sticks.

"Brett, these sticks are bad."

"They're fine, Dad."

"Son, you need more curve."

"Hey, fifty-eight goals or seventy-two goals?"

"I scored seventy-seven goals one season, for the Winnipeg Jets"

"In the NHL ... your fifty-eight or my seventy-two?"

Dad roared with his hoarse laughter. "OK, you got me there. You can have the stick back."

Actually, it's rare that I try to play one-up with Dad — no matter how long I play hockey, I won't be able to match his accomplishments. He was a fifty-goal scorer when you could still count them on one hand. Three times, players scored exactly fifty goals — but Dad was the first to score more than fifty, when he netted fifty-four in 1965-66. He had thirty or more goals for seventeen consecutive seasons in the NHL and WHA. He won the NHL scoring title three times.

Dad said fans were his motivation to play hard every game. "You never want to come out of a dressing room after a game and have no one waiting for you," he says. "If there is no one waiting for your autograph, it probably means you haven't done anything."

Even opposing players respected Dad. Berry remembers getting cut severely at Chicago Stadium and meeting Dad for the first time.

Berry, playing for the Los Angeles Kings, was skating behind the Blackhawks' net, when Chicago defenseman Keith Magnuson's stick ended up in his eye on the follow-through.

"I really thought I was going to lose my eye," Berry said. "They brought me into the Blackhawks' medical room and started to stitch me up. I remember someone coming in and grasping my hand and saying, 'Don't worry, kid, you're going to be all right.' It turned out to be Bobby Hull. I don't think I'll every forget that."

Dad also likes to laugh, including at himself. He loves to tell stories, though he insists he's starting to forget his best ones. "I'm getting older now," he says with a laugh. "And when you get old, three things happen. First, you lose your memory ... and I can't remember the other two."

Dad's wit was sharp when he went to the All-Star Game in Chicago last season, to watch me play. An oldtimers' game was part of the festivities, and he also filled out that SportsChannel America questionnaire. He saw a chance to poke fun at his third-oldest son. He took it.

One of the questions was: Do you have any relative playing hockey?

Dad wrote, "My son, Bobby Jr., plays in a midnight league, and my wife likes to put the pads on now and then."

ST. LOUIS

Chapter 16

Not Dead, Just Sleeping

A seventy-two-year-old St. Louis grandmother writes me twice every month, to tell me I'm the sexiest man this side of Bob Barker.

I've gotten up to four hundred letters a day from all over the world. It seems like I've heard from everyone except Elvis, which leads me to believe he really might be dead. Soviet Union. Poland. Czechoslovakia. Finland. Germany. My mail is a geography lesson. At the end of last season, one letter arrived with a Japanese postmark, and a postal service employee attached a sticker to the envelope: "Way to go, Brett, this must be your first from Japan!"

Women write and ask me to marry them. And a guy I never met wanted me to attend his son's bar mitzvah. One fellow from Saskatoon sent me an invitation to come to his Saskatoon gas station, for an auction of a Brett Hull rookie hockey card. Sorry, I can't make that one.

The grandmother of Chicago Blackhawks centre Jeremy Roenick even wrote and said she wanted to meet me.

One gentleman requested my favorite recipe, to include in a celebrity seafood cookbook. He got my recipe for Brett's Barbecue Tuna Steaks. My tuna made the cut, along with the Australian Prime Minister's swordfish and Bill Cosby's seafood specialty. We'll assume Bill serves Jello pudding for dessert with that.

Being a celebrity is an interesting mix of fun and weirdness. Truthfully, it's really difficult to comprehend. I always think, *Who, me? You want my autograph, my tuna recipe, my stick, my endorsement of your product?* Is this the same me who couldn't get an invitation from a junior hockey team when he was seventeen years old?

It still amazes me when I come out of St. Louis Arena forty-five minutes after a game, and find fifty people waiting for my autograph. During a playoff game in Minnesota, I was besieged by so many fans that the team was almost late for its chartered flight. The following game, I had to sneak out with the equipment truck just so I wouldn't inconvenience the team. Ten years ago, no one wanted me. Now, I'm twenty-seven, and the hockey world can't get enough of me. It's difficult to understand. I still see myself as an average guy, battling to keep my weight down and my bank account up. Just like everyone else.

Fans have even found my house. Kids leave notes on my door. "Joe and I rode our bikes over here, but we missed you. We'll catch you next time."

None of this bothers me, because fans are what the game is all about. My dad taught me that. No hockey player ever treated fans with more respect than my father. His charisma draws fans like Kelly Chase draws penalties.

The scenario was the same, whether it was Chicago or Winnipeg. Dad and family would be walking down the street. Then someone would recognize him. He would sign one autograph after another. Eventually, he would be surrounded by a crowd. He would disappear behind a wall of fans. He kept signing until everyone was gone.

"Athletes are nothing without their fans," Dad told his kids. "Fans keep the sport alive. We owe them an effort on and off the ice."

Hopefully, I've maintained a similar attitude. Here's what I do: sign every autograph request I receive in the mail, and each one that's humanly possible when I'm approached at the rink.

Here's what I don't do: accept money to attend card-collecting shows and sign autographs. I think it's wrong to charge kids for autographs.

The whole memorabilia craze has gotten way out of hand. I signed a contract with Scoreboard Inc. to distribute official Hull-autographed items, such as sweaters, sticks, pictures, etc. I did it to provide some legitimate avenue for fans to acquire items, rather than to make a pile of money.

International Management Group Vice-President Michael Barnett, who became my agent when Goodenow went to the NHL Players' Association, got his hands on some pictures being represented, and sold, as autographed by Wayne Gretzky and Brett Hull. It was obvious the autographs were fake. There was no attempt to make the forgery look authentic. A twelve-year-old could have done a better job.

Barnett, who also represents Gretzky, decided that if someone went after the originator of bogus material, it could discourage others from distributing it.

He followed a trail that led him through many card and memorabilia shops around the United States. One shop had purchased the pictures from another, which had received them from a small distributor. Barnett played detective until he traced the source to a major dealer in New York.

When Barnett confronted him, the dealer proclaimed innocence.

"I bought those photographs from a ten-year-old kid who hangs around the rink," he told Mike. "The kid gets to know all the players, and they sign them for him."

Mike couldn't believe what he was hearing. "How can you possibly believe that Wayne or Brett might sign fifty photos for a kid?" Mike said.

The dealer had no answer except to say that he took the kid at his word.

There you have it — the integrity of a million-dollar industry came down to the word of a ten-year-old kid with an unbelievable story. It makes you wonder.

Most of the correspondence I receive could be classified as happy mail. Mostly from autograph-seekers or fans who just want to wish me luck. But I also occasionally receive a letter or two that keeps hockey in the proper perspective. The Blues have set up one desk to handle the deluge of mail I receive each day.

One basket has been set aside for special letters — those determined by team vice-president Susie Mathieu to need immediate attention.

One such letter came from a father from the St. Louis suburb of St. Charles. He was fighting a custody battle over his son, and confided in me the boy had been abused by his estranged wife. He believed that, if he could arrange for the boy to meet me, it might play some tiny role in helping him deal with the trauma.

We invited him to the next home game, and it turned out this kid was the absolute greatest. Now, we are the best of buddies.

His father recently wrote to tell me he won the custody battle. It made my day. Some wins are far more significant than those I'm trying to achieve on the ice. The father took a picture of his son and me and had it made into a calendar. It's hanging on my refrigerator.

The saddest letters are from teen-agers who don't seem to have anyone left to talk to, except me. I've been a happy-go-lucky person my entire life. It bothers me to see young people with so many troubles.

There was a particularly emotional one from a seventeen-year-old girl who had dropped out of school. She had stopped speaking to her mother. Her dad worked so much that he stopped noticing she was alive.

How do you answer a letter like that? All I could tell her was that she should rethink the value of education, and try to talk to her family — or her pastor, or school counselor if that wasn't an option. Somehow, that didn't seem like enough. It's frustrating to be powerless. I'm trained to be a right wing, not a counselor.

I faithfully write a few extra lines to letter-writing kids whose parents are divorcing. I went through that myself, and I know it can be a difficult adjustment. I just remind the kids their parents are divorcing each other; they aren't divorcing their children. The other important thing I remind them of is that they have nothing to do with the parents' problems.

Learning to cope with fame probably has been aided by my growing friendship with Wayne Gretzky.

Barnett called me once, to offer me a business option. He explained Tiger Electronics wanted to manufacture a one-on-one hockey game, similar to a one-on-one basketball game featuring Magic Johnson and Larry Bird.

Basically, the deal was that Tiger Electronics was willing to pay me a wad of money to lend my name to a one-on-one game with Gretzky.

I just stopped Mike in mid-sentence. "I'm in," I said. "I would pay *them* to be on a game with Wayne Gretzky."

Wayne is an awesome guy. We spent some time together this summer, filming a commercial, then hanging out at a Toronto Argos CFL game. Later in the summer (when my Team USA and Gretz's Team Canada were in Saskatoon), we were both supposed to be watching Canada play Czechoslovakia in an exhibition game. Gretzky was sitting out that game, so we ducked out after the first period to get something to eat and watch the Gretzky-owned Argos play on television. It was like ditching school with the class president.

He's given me some advice on endorsements — like avoiding companies that only seem interested in a quick hit. He also warned me about the danger of spreading yourself so thin that your off-season becomes non-existent. I got a taste of that this season. Between commercials, projects and Canada Cup, the summer was gone.

No one knows how to handle fame, or does it better, than Gretzky. He's had to deal with it since he was about ten. I've only had to cope with it since I scored seventy-two goals.

One aspect of my life has changed, since I've established myself in the NHL. I dress better. Mom always worked in the fashion business, and my clothes choices drove her nuts. She bought me my first suit when I was Harry's best man. She had to bribe me with cowboy boots, to get me to wear it. My friends will tell you that a suit on me in those days was like seeing earrings on a pig.

Last season, when the St. Louis Blues were playing in Vancouver, Adam Oates and I went shopping at A.E. Lee, an exclusive clothing store. We got there just at closing time. The manager, perhaps recognizing who we were, unlocked the door to let us in. I went wild, buying a suit and a few shirts. The final bill was $3,500.

When Mom visited me in St. Louis and saw a "Thank-you" fax from A.E. Lee, she beamed like a mom whose son had just received his first *A* on his report card.

"All this time, I thought I raised a country bumpkin," she quipped.

Mom is the one who seems to be having the most fun with my celebrity status. She will stop in hockey card shops just to check out the cost of my rookie card. "When they start explaining why your card is so much, I get a kick out telling them, 'Oh, I know all about him, because I'm his mom.'"

Mom and Harry also had right wing Trevor Linden living with them, during his rookie season with the Vancouver Canucks. Brian Burke, who is now a Canucks vice-president, asked her if Trevor, who was eighteen at the time, could stay for a couple of months. But it worked out so well that Trevor stayed the whole season. He and Bart, who also was a teenager then, became good friends.

When the Blues were in town to play the Canucks, I also stayed at the house. Mom found it amusing to "have two Number Sixteens sitting down and having dinner together, knowing tomorrow you'll be going out and trying to beat each other," she said.

I turned to Trevor and said, "Yeah, so don't hurt me, you big lug." Trevor is 6-foot-4, 205 pounds.

My family very much enjoyed having Linden. He became a member of the family. Bart even complained that Linden received the same number of Christmas presents as he did. Mom missed him when he moved out in his second year. "He should have continued to stay with us," Mom joked, "because he didn't play as well in the second season as he did in the first season."

The whole celebrity aspect of my life boggles my mind. Some of the requests I receive are so unbelievable that I'm wary someone will be able to pull off a practical joke at my expense. The first time I was told

David Letterman wanted me to appear on his show, I was sure it was my teammates' idea of a prank. Susie Mathieu convinced me it was legitimate. I depend on Susie so much to keep track of my commitments that if she ever decides to pull a fast one, I'm dead meat.

But there I was getting ready to go on the Letterman show, along with legendary drummer Ginger Baker. They did my makeup next to Tony Randall. Talk about your odd couple. It was the greatest, even though I'm sure Tony had no idea who I was.

I've appeared on *Arsenio Hall*, *Good Morning America*, *Canada A.M.*. But appearing on David Letterman was the most fun, probably because when I was in college, *Late Night with David Letterman* was standard fare for my friends. I like his schtick. I enjoy his irreverence. I like the way he pokes fun at General Electric, the owner of NBC, the network that airs his show. I also enjoyed it, because I scored with a couple of one-liners.

Letterman is one of the few hosts I have met who doesn't want to spend the whole time talking about hockey. Most of them want to ask what it feels like to score goals, or what I think about Wayne Gretzky, or what it's like to be the NHL's premier goal-scorer. Well, it would be a lot more interesting, if you would ask me about something other than hockey.

Letterman talked about drivers in Missouri. There are some poor drivers in the Show Me state. It's a subject I can relate to.

Of course, he tried to zing me. "You're going to get all this money, but you still have work in St. Louis."

"It beats working for GE," I said.

He liked that. So did the studio audience.

Next time, he asked me if I had all my own teeth. "I know your dad didn't have all his," he said.

"I can go one better than that," I said. "I have all my own teeth and all my own hair." He liked that. No word about what Dad had to say about it.

It's great fun being in the limelight and meeting celebrities. It makes me think it would be the coolest to be a movie star. I met soap opera star Jack Wagner at a celebrity golf tournament in Lake Tahoe, Nevada. He's from St. Louis, and we hit it off pretty well. He said he would try to get me on the television show, *Santa Barbara.*

I'd be a great actor. But doing love scenes — that could be weird. Maybe I should do Westerns. I could be a cowboy. That would be awesome. Think about it. Me and Clint riding off into the sunset.

One thing my dad could do, that I probably never will be able to do, is use celebrity influence at restaurants, shows and things like that. Mostly, I fear rejection. I'm afraid they'll say, "Brett who?"

The only time I used my celebrity status was to get backstage to see Canadian-born Neil Young after a concert. His father, Scott Young, who wrote for the Toronto *Globe & Mail*, is in the Hockey Hall of Fame as a sportswriter. We had a good time talking hockey.

Neil knows hockey. But his band members have better taste in music than they do in teams; they're Chicago Blackhawks fans.

My teammates enjoy poking fun at my celebrity status. Once, as my girlfriend, Alison Curran, waited for me after a game, she asked my former teammate Sergio Momesso where I was.

"Oh, God is still getting dressed," he said, with a huge grin.

After that, I was the subject of a month's-worth of diety jokes. Considering how much I disliked my other, less-blasphemous nicknames, you can imagine what I thought of that one.

Once, Kelly Chase came to me with a request. He wanted to order stick blades for Steve Tuttle and himself. I knew their blades were the same lie as mine, but I didn't know why they wanted me to order them.

"Because," Chaser said, "if Brett Hull orders sticks, they'll show up tomorrow by Purolator Courier. If Kelly Chase orders sticks, they'll look at the order; 'He doesn't score goals, we can send those out in about three or four weeks.'"

Of course I placed the order because, when I was a nobody in Calgary, I think they sent my sticks aboard the slow boat from China.

Speaking of sticks, one season's supply for me now is about four hundred. No, I don't break as many as I used to, because I switched to an Easton aluminum shaft. But I get so many requests for sticks, from charities and opposing teams' players, that I average about four or five a game. This costs the Blues more than $20,000 a year.

You know memorabilia-collecting is widespread, when even the players are into it. During the post-game handshake after the Norris Division playoff final, Brian Bellows asked me if he could have my stick for a keepsake. Sure, why not?

Alison is perhaps my best ally for keeping my life and career in proper perspective. She represents the voice of reason in my life. I need that, because I only see the positive in everything. She's also there to give me a push, which I need regularly. I'll be lounging around on the sofa during the summer, and she'll say, "Why don't you get up and go out and do some running, before training camp."

Brian Sutter should put her on the staff (along with that bear in Duluth), because both have a way of getting me to run.

Alison is a superb athlete — a top-level softball player and a former youth league goaltender. Mike Cortes, who played with me at Minnesota-Duluth, was her backup when they played together as kids.

Alison's dad owned a tavern in Duluth and was a car dealer. When Mom heard that, she said, "Leave it to Brett to find a girlfriend who is a former goal-tender, with a father who owns a bar and an auto dealership."

I'm a partner in a St. Louis restaurant. As part of the deal, I have input into the menu. That isn't as dangerous as it may seem. I actually have quite a bit of knowledge about food. I like to eat plenty of it — and I'm non-discriminatory. I like it all.

After I returned to Duluth last June, I asked Susie Mathieu to check on my home in St. Louis. I asked her to remove all the food from my refrigerator.

She called me later that day. "Brett, I found thirty-six boxes of Girl Scout cookies in your refrigerator."

What did she think she was going to find? A head of lettuce and tofu? I eat all-American, cholesterol-enriched food. It seems like every Girl Scout in the Greater St. Louis Metropolitan Area was sent out with a case of cookies and directions to Brett Hull's house.

The strangest situation in my nouveau celebrity status occurred a few days after I had signed my $7.1 million contract. Susie got a call that nearly brought her to tears.

"Susie, this is Tom Ryther of KSTP Television in Minneapolis. We just got word that Brett Hull was seriously injured in a car accident last night, and is in a local hospital here. Can you confirm this?."

Susie was stunned. "I can't confirm it, but I can't deny it, either."

I had left two days before, saying I was headed for Duluth. At that point, I didn't own a home there. Susie didn't know exactly where I intended to stay when I got there.

She called Tonto about ten times. She left messages with increasing urgency on the answering machine. She called Goodenow. He had no clue where I was. She called Mom, all my brothers and every other number she had in her phone book.

Susie, by this time, was mortified. She is a close friend, and she had all but convinced herself that I had been out celebrating my contract with friends and fallen asleep behind the wheel while listening to some mellow Bob Dylan song.

And just to make the situation more interesting, she knew the team had yet to insure my contract. I was scheduled for a physical in Boston in a few days. If I was medically cleared, the Blues would be insured in the event I suffered a career-ending injury. If I was toast before then, the Blues would get burned for $7.1 million.

She finally went in to tell Quinn of the possibility I'd been maimed in some mishap.

Right then, her office phone rang.

"Susie, it's Brett."

"Brett, where have you been?"

"I've been sleeping. I just got up, and there're a hundred messages from you on Tonto's machine."

She told me the whole story, and we theorized that a license plate that had been stolen from my car two weeks before, in Duluth, was probably at the bottom of the confusion. We never knew for sure.

"Well, thank God you're alive. I have to call everyone and tell them you're all right."

"Nah, let the story ride for a while," I said.

Susie didn't think that was quite as funny as I did.

ST. LOUIS

CHAPTER 17

LIVE
FROM
PORCUPINE
PLAIN

Dressing room humor is as much a part of hockey as ugly defensemen and chipped teeth.

Walking through the Blues' dressing room is like a tour through Animal House; one-liners home in on targets with the relentless pursuit of a cruise missile. Life is a ribbing session. Zinging teammates is almost a form of relaxation. It's a long season. It's a pressure release. Nobody gets offended; I should know, because I'm one of the favorite targets. I like to give as much as I receive.

Sometimes it's just silly stuff, like calling Paul Cavallini "Wally Wall Street," because he reads the *Wall Street Journal*.

When defenseman Robert Dirk scored his second goal, and first two-point game, of a career going back to 1987-88, Blues goaltender Curtis Joseph joked, "Now that Dirk has all this offensive prowess, we'll have to find a stay-at-home defenseman to play with Dirk."

If I'm not fooling around, I go crazy. Whenever I'm feeling too serious, I start to worry that I'm too uptight to play. I feel like I have to do something to stay loose. Maybe it's something short and sweet, like gently flicking pucks at someone's back during practice, or something long and sustained like exchanging zingers with one of the many worthy dressing-room opponents.

"Hullie," Oatsie said to me, "you have this incredible way of cutting up people without them geting mad at you. No one ever feels insulted. It's the smile."

One day, word got around that a Miss Something-or-Another contest had requested a date with Kelly Chase, who is from the bustling metropolis of Porcupine Plain, Saskatchewan.

That lob was too easy not to slam.

"Chaser, I don't understand why she would want a date with you," I said, matter-of-factly.

"And why not?" Chaser said, going along with the obvious joke.

"Because you're ugly, of course," I said.

"And who should they want?"

"Well, I already have Alison, so I wouldn't go. But they should ask me."

"Why should they want you? You're certainly no beauty yourself. You're uglier than I am."

"That's true. But I'm rich."

My contract is one of the favorite subjects of the dressing room comedians. The Blues deliver mail in one of those big manila envelopes. Every time it comes into the room, Gino Cavallini says an envelope that size must have my paycheque in it.

If our cheques come late, then someone will say it's because they can't afford to pay anybody except me.

Every time we're in a restaurant, the guys tell me to pick up the tab. Of course I tell them, "I wouldn't pick up the tab if I made $10 million per year."

One of my better moments of humor came at a team golf outing on a payday. We were on the green, and I had to mark my ball. I was searching my pockets unsuccessfully for a ball marker or a coin, when it hit me. I whipped out my paycheque and set it down in place of my ball. The guys hooted like crazy. The break of the green was right to left over the last zero in my paycheque.

Guys like Chaser, Darin Kimble, Mario Marois are quick with the one-liners. Ron Wilson had one of the best last season.

It was at the end of practice one day, and tough guys Kimble and Glen Featherstone were down in the corner, talking. The rest of us were shooting around, as Wilson spotted Kimble and Featherstone. Said Wilson, "What are the chances those two are talking about calculus?"

Got 'em.

Chaser gets into verbal jousts on the ice all the time. One of his verbal attacks was so sharp-witted it was carried in just about every paper in Canada and the United States. His mom heard about it in Saskatchewan. That got him in trouble.

He had been in another fight against Van Dorp and, when it was over, Chaser got in one final shot while the linesmen had Van Dorp tied up. Van Dorp became enraged. He had a felony in mind. They ended up in the penalty box with Van Dorp still screaming and throwing things at him. Eventually, the referee threw them both out of the game.

The next day, Riendeau asked Chaser why Van Dorp, whom Chaser always refers to as a cement-head, was screaming at him. "I don't know, Vinnie," Chaser said. "I'm not fluent in cement."

A reporter heard the comment and used it in the newspaper. Because reporters trade notes like they were commodities on the stock exchange, Chase's witticism appeared in print. Chaser got a call from his good friend Wendel Clark, asking him about the comment. He also got a call from his mother. A grinning Chaser said, "Mom told me if I can't say anything nice about someone, I shouldn't say anything."

Once, when Mario Marois and I were getting on the bus, he glanced up and saw Cavallini, Featherstone, Kimble and Wilson playing cards. Without missing a beat, he said, "Brett, look over there. If you put these four heads together, you've got a good start to a rock pile."

Got 'em.

One of my favorite shots came when we were short of pucks during a practice. I always look to Kimble and Chaser, who aren't exactly known to be smooth shooters. "Why don't you two go over there and shoot for a while," I said. "You'll hack those three pucks into about ten. Then we'll have plenty."

Got 'em.

Chaser gets me regularly. "Hey, Hullie," he says, "I got the perfect title for your book. It should be called, *From Fat to Fame: The Brett Hull Story.*"

Teammates make hockey enjoyable. There is nothing better than hanging out with the guys. I have always been fortunate to be surrounded by great guys, everywhere I've played.

Here's a comment or two about players I've known along the way.

◇

Minnesota-Duluth Bulldogs (1984-86)
Matt Christensen: A close friend who would have been one of the finest players the Blues ever had.

Jim Toninato: My best friend.

Bill Watson (retired from NHL): He's one of the greatest collegiate hockey players of all time. He had the best hands I ever saw.

Norm Maciver (now with the Edmonton Oilers): The second-best passer I ever played with. He has gone unnoticed for too long.

Dave Cowan: He was my centre as a freshman, and helped me get where I am today.

Skeeter Moore: Did all the work for my goals in college.

Jimmy Johnson (now with the Minnesota North Stars): His success speaks for itself.

Moncton Golden Flames 1986-87

Randy Burridge (now with the Washington Capitals): He was my left wing when I scored fifty goals.

Doug Kostynski (playing in Europe): He helped build my scoring confidence.

Bob Sweeney (now with the Boston Bruins): He's the funniest teammate I ever had. He doesn't get a lot of goals — but they are always the prettiest.

Gary Roberts (now with Calgary Flames): One of my better friends around the league.

Brian Bradley (now with Toronto Maple Leafs): He was the rebel of Moncton.

Kraig Nienhaus: He was really Terry Crisp's whipping boy.

Doug Dadswell (now with New Jersey Devils): We were roommates in Calgary, thank God.

Calgary Flames 1986-88

Joe Mullen (now with Pittsburgh Penguins): What a great guy. I copied his stick pattern when I first came to the NHL.

Al MacInnis: He could use one hand, and still blister the puck harder than I can.

Paul Reinhart (now retired): What an awesome talent.

Mike Bullard (now with the Toronto Maple Leafs): He was the centre on what we called the "What the Bleep" line. I was the right wing.

John Tonelli (unconditional free agent): He was the left wing on the "What the Bleep" line.

Carey Wilson (free agent): Terrific hands. He's a long-time family friend. My brother, Bobby Jr., was best man at his wedding.

Joel Otto: Go, Twins, Go. He loves his baseball.

Jim Peplinski (now a hockey analyst for CBC): They call him Pepper. He treated me like a king as a rookie. I'll never forget that.

Lanny McDonald (now retired): Hall of Famer.

Gary Suter: One of the NHL's most underrated defensemen.

Jamie Macoun (now with the Toronto Maple Leafs): Near the top of my list of defensemen I hate to play against.

Hakan Loob (playing in Europe): An unbelievable ping pong player.

Colin Patterson: No one works harder than this man. I got my chance in Calgary when he pulled a hamstring.

Tim Hunter: Sat next to me in the Flames' dressing room. He's the kind of player who has worked for everything he has.

Neil Sheehy (now back with the Calgary Flames): One of a kind.

Dan Quinn (now with the Philadelphia Flyers): My first centre man. Excellent golfer.

Perry Berezan (now with the San Jose Sharks): Call him Wheels.

Nick Fotiu (now retired): He loved to tell me Bobby Hull stories.

Doug Risebrough (now general manager): Riser is the ultimate blue collar worker.

Joe Nieuwendyk: Newy is the only guy I've ever

seen score four goals with only one being a shot on net. He's a close friend. He's one of the few guys I've seen who seems to have as much fun as I do on the ice.

Paul Baxter (fired as assistant coach after 1991-92 season): Another tremendous guy, who helped me break into the National Hockey League.

Mike Vernon: I'll take him as my goaltender any time, any place, any league. When I skate by him during games, he always says, "Still lucky, eh, kid?"

Brad McCrimmon (now with the Detroit Red Wings): This guy has more nicknames than I have goals. Sergeant Carter is my favorite.

Craig Coxe (finished 1991-92 with Kalamazoo, Mich., of the IHL): A happy-go-lucky guy. "Happy Days" is his favorite expression.

Brian Glynn (now with Edmonton Oilers): He was the only guy on the Flames who sat out as much as I did.

Ric Nattress (now with the Toronto Maple Leafs): Awesome guy.

St. Louis Blues (1988 to present)

Peter Zezel (now with the Toronto Maple Leafs): You don't score seventy-two goals without having a good centre like Zezel.

Bernie Federko (now retired): He taught me plenty about the game and the "pride of the Blue Note."

Cliff Ronning (now playing with the Vancouver Canucks): He needs to learn to accept a compliment.

Greg Paslawski (now with the Quebec Nordiques): Funny, funny guy. Steve Martin on skates.

Tony Hrkac (now with the Chicago Blackhawks): Mr. Good Times/Bad Times.

Gino Cavallini (now with the Quebec Nordiques): Another close friend.

Tony McKegney (played in Italy 1991-92): The only guy I know who can score forty goals and still get traded. Why, Tony?

Rick Meagher (now coaching Peoria in the IHL): Fastest man alive. His speed is ludicrous.

Sergio Momesso (now playing with the Vancouver Canucks): I wish he was still playing in St. Louis. We had great times together.

Gordie Roberts (Now with the Pittsburgh Penguins): He's a trainer's nightmare.

Steve Tuttle (playing for Peoria in IHL): Quietest guy I ever met.

Paul Cavallini: Call him J.B.E., or Junior Business Executive.

Tom Tilley (playing in Europe): Never really got a chance.

Doug Evans (now with the Boston Bruins): Whitey is one of the few guys I've met who can get right under someone's skin.

Herb Raglan (now with the Quebec Nordiques): Close friend. One of the hardest hitters I know.

Gaston Gingras (playing in Europe): Pea shooter.

Mario Marois: He's one of the few guys in this league who has more fun playing hockey than I do.

Todd Ewen (now with the Montreal Canadiens): The Gentle Giant.

Dave Lowry: The Blues wouldn't be the same without him.

Glen Featherstone (now with the Boston Bruins): Another comedian. His future is in his own hands.

Robert Dirk (now with the Vancouver Canucks): I've never seen him lose a fight.

Vincent Riendeau (now with the Detroit Red Wings): Bonjour, Vinnie.

Greg Millen (free agent): One of the league's finest gentleman. He deserves the world on a platter.

Paul MacLean (now Blues' pro scout): Call him Mac. After Sudsy and Bob, he's my mentor.

Rod Brind'Amour (now with the Philadelphia Flyers): Best body I've seen in hockey. I think it inhibits his play.

Ron Wilson: Dog.

Rich Sutter: I wish there were nineteen Rich Sutters on the Blues.

Scott Stevens: A heart and soul player.

Harold Snepsts (assistant coach): After watching him play, I now understand how he played for sixteen years.

Curtis Joseph: Destined for greatness.

Pat Jablonski: One of the league's hardest workers.

Garth Butcher: You don't appreciate him until you play with him.

Bob Bassen: Scud.

Geoff Courtnall (now with the Vancouver Canucks): Forehand or backhand, no one better.

CHAPTER 18

OH, CANADA

I pledged allegiance to a team — not a flag — when I decided to play for Team USA in the Canada Cup Tournament.

My decision was about loyalty, not nationalism or patriotism. In 1986, U.S. national team coach Dave Peterson and Canadian national team coach Dave King both watched me play for Minnesota-Duluth. King didn't think I could skate well enough to play for Canada. Team USA general manager Art Berglund and Peterson invited me to play for Team USA in the World Championships in Moscow.

When Team Canada and Team USA both sent me an invitation to play for their Canada Cup teams, my choice seemed simple. And despite what everyone seems to believe, Wayne Gretzky made no attempt to talk me into playing for Canada. There was no promise to be his right wing. He never said a word about my decision. He knows me well enough to know I believe in loyalty. I don't care if I was born in Belleville, Ontario, Chicago or Moscow. The Americans took me in 1986. So I owed them in 1991.

I'm amazed everyone takes Canada Cup nationalism so seriously. I never viewed it as Canada vs. USA. I *HATE* the whole anthem aspect of the tournament. We're not going to war; we're playing hockey. To me, it was two good teams playing against each other in high-tempo hockey. It was a chance for the world's best professional players from Sweden, Finland, Czechoslovakia, the Soviet Union, the USA and Canada to showcase their skills in a highly competitive atmosphere. Right wing is my hockey position, not a statement of my political beliefs. I went looking for good hockey, not global supremacy for my country.

What I took home from the tournament was a greater appreciation of the talent level in the NHL. We all know the NHL has plenty of talent — but it's more noticible when it's all gathered in one tournament. Some of the lesser-known players get a chance to show their ability. For example, take Washington Capitals forward Kevin Miller. I didn't know how gifted he was, until I saw him play at this level. He's got some nifty moves. If the Capitals give him half a chance, he might be an outstanding player.

I think fans believe hockey players know everything about every team. But you have to remember that with expansion there are twelve teams I am going to see only twice a year. I really didn't know what a solid defenseman New Jersey Devils' Eric Weinrich was until I played with him in the Canada

Cup. Just what I need, another talented defenseman to worry about. One person who didn't surprise me — but may have surprised some fans — was Minnesota North Stars defenseman Jim Johnson. We were teammates at Minnesota-Duluth. He was a gritty, high-quality defenseman then, and nothing has changed. He had an excellent tournament.

An interesting aspect of these tournaments is that, for four or five weeks, you are friends with guys whom you couldn't stand during the regular season. Chicago Blackhawks Chris Chelios will probably try to check me into the fourth row when we play this season; but we were good buddies in the tournament. The same goes for his Blackhawks teammate, Jeremy Roenick, and the Minnesota North Stars' Mike Modano. Don't tell Sudsy that I hung around with my Norris Division enemies.

My Team USA teammates were about as fun-loving as my Blues brothers. We had a particularly good time in Chicago, with Roenick and Chelios as tour guides. Included on our expedition was a trip to historic Wrigley Field. We were invited into the Cubs' dressing room. Cubs first baseman Mark Grace, a big hockey fan, gave me a bat. I don't know which of us was more impressed to meet the other.

While, we were in Chicago, reporters asked me about my scoring drought. I finished the tournament tied for the team scoring lead, with nine points. But I only had two goals in eight games. Everyone wanted to know why I wasn't scoring goals. I tried to come up with a logical answer: I missed Oatsie. Sounded good to me.

I said I figured I wouldn't get my game back together until I got back to St. Louis. I said I had some difficulty adjusting to not having Adam Oates as my centre. He always knows exactly where I'm at and what I'm planning to do. It's like he's inside my head, watching my thought pattern.

I think my final quote in the paper was, "When I

play with Oatsie, I'm playing with a guy whose only thought is passing me the puck."

When I skated on the ice for the next day's practice, Pat LaFontaine had taped the name OATES on his back. Joel Otto had done the same. I love dressing-room humor.

Assistant coach Jay Leach was another funny guy. He used to feed me the puck for my shooting drill at the end of practice. After each puck, he'd yell, "Oates to Hull. Goal!" Obviously, he wanted me to feel comfortable.

To be truthful, nobody felt comfortable right after Bob Johnson had emergency surgery to remove a malignant brain tumor, on August 29. It was two days before the opening game against Sweden, in Pittsburgh. We were all stunned. Some of the guys had noticed Bob didn't look well; Gary Suter said a reporter had mentioned to him that Bob had been slurring his words. A lot of guys knew he had complained of fatigue, but had attributed it to the long road trip we had just endured. Some guys close to him found out when he went into surgery after midnight. Others, like me, didn't find out until we showed up for practice the next day.

The news overwhelmed some players, particularly those who had played for him in the NHL. I knew Bob from Calgary, but I really only played a few games for him. The year I spent in Moncton was his last season with the Flames. But in the one training and few games I played for him, he was one of the most outgoing, positive-thinking coaches I've ever met. He was also a big believer in college players. After all, he was the man who allowed me to play my first NHL game, in the Stanley Cup final in 1985-86.

I didn't know him nearly as well as Gary Suter, Joel Otto and Joe Mullen, who had spent several seasons with him. Mullen was almost like another of Bob's sons. When Bob came back to the NHL before last season, he asked Penguins general manager

Craig Patrick to acquire Joe from Calgary. Mullen said repeatedly that it was difficult for him to concentrate on playing.

Suter was eight when he started going to Johnson's coaching clinics. He and Chelios played for the University of Wisconsin Badgers when Johnson coached there. In fifteen years at Wisconsin, Johnson won three NCAA titles.

Pat LaFontaine made the point that everyone on the team had probably been affected by Johnson in one way or another in their careers. Bob Johnson, nicknamed "Badger Bob," *is* American hockey. Before he coached the Pittsburgh Penguins to their first-ever Stanley Cup championship last spring, he was executive director of USA's amateur program. Johnson coached the Calgary Flames from 1982 to 1987, taking them to the Stanley Cup finals in 1985-86.

The surgery left him temporarily paralyzed and unable to speak. Yet, less than thirty-six hours after surgery, he wrote out a gameplan from his bed at Mercy Hospital, which was across the street from the Pittsburgh Civic Center.

"His mind's as sharp as ever," Team USA general manager Craig Patrick told us. "He wrote the lineup out ... and the strategy to deal with the Swedish forechecking."

Everyone was real quiet the day of the first game; we didn't need any pre-game pep talk. We took a 5-0 lead and won 6-3. Mullen said afterward he could barely keep his mind on the game. Sweden's Ulf Samuelsson, who played for Johnson in Pittsburgh, said the outcome didn't matter.

"Winning and losing just aren't that important anymore," Samuelsson said. Even the crowd of more than 13,000 was unusually quiet.

Pittsburgh Penguins winger Kevin Stevens, who didn't play in the tournament because he was negotiating a new contract, visited Johnson in Pittsburgh while Team USA jetted to Hamilton, Ontario, for a Monday game against Canada.

As soon as Stevens entered the room, Johnson scribbled out a note that said, "Get on a plane and go to Hamilton."

I really expected nothing less from Bob. He is an amazing man, with such a burning desire to coach. You can tell that just by the fact that he came back to coach in the NHL at age sixty. He's a fighter.

We lost 6-3 to Canada in a physical game; we actually outplayed the Canadians in the final period-and-a-half. Then, we beat the Czechs 4-2. Our biggest win was a 2-1 decision against the Soviets in a loud Chicago Stadium. The win put Team USA in the semifinal, for the first time since 1984.

It was the first time an American team recorded a major tournament win against a Soviet hockey team, since the 1980 Olympics in Lake Placid.

USA was 0-5 against the Soviets in previous Canada Cup games. The loss put the Soviets out of a tournament medal round, for the first time in their hockey history.

Canada had tied the Finns 2-2, and the Soviets 3-3. Canada had been in danger of losing against the Soviets; Brent Sutter scored with only 5:16 remaining, to tie the game. At completion of the preliminary round, USA (4-1) and Canada (3-0-2) were tied with eight points. Canada was seeded first.

In the semifinal, it was Canada vs. Sweden and USA vs. Finland. Through a scheduling coincidence, we also had to play them in the last game of the preliminary round. We defeated the Finns 4-3 in the meaningless game, in which neither side wanted to show much of its potential.

A win against the Finns in the semifinal, two nights later, would mean USA's first trip to a Canada Cup final. The significance of that achievement was brought home by a man whose whole life had been dedicated to American hockey. At the pregame dinner before the game against Finland, a fax from Bob Johnson was read:

Dear coaches and players:

Congratulations!

When we started training camp, the medal round was our goal. That time has finally arrived.

In athletics, all you get is one chance and that is what we have now. You are representing all Americans — including all the little kids who are playing the great game of hockey. For all the kids in the border towns from Minnesota to New York — you are their heroes. All the hockey kids idolize Gretzky. I want them to idolize players like Roenick and Modano from the US.

USA Hockey needs identity. This is our chance to reach out for some.

I wish I was going to be on the plane to Hamilton today.

Good Luck

Bob

LaFontaine just shook his head. "With all he's going through, and he's still thinking about us."

Fittingly, Joey Mullen scored twice, as we defeated the Finns 7-3. Dave Christain, Kevin Miller, Joel Otto, Doug Brown and Brian Leetch scored one goal each. Leetch played a great game on defense.

Team USA official Art Berglund told us he called Johnson at the hospital with updates. "When he heard the news, he gave the thumbs-up," Berglund said.

Canada defeated Sweden 4-0, to assure the dream matchup. The USA vs. Canada final had been predicted from the beginning. During January's All-Star break, Wayne Gretzky said he feared the American team more than any other.

Brian Sutter, an assistant coach for Canada, told me Canada picked its team to play against USA in the final. Mike Keenan and his staff correctly assumed we would be there.

That doesn't explain to me why Oatsie got cut from Team Canada. That's just a crime. Then, Steve Yzerman didn't make it. Another crime. Canada's coaches decided to use more grinders, with the hopes of dominating USA along the boards. Team USA, deeper in talent than it had been in the past, still only had a few players who played a physical game.

We lost Game One to Canada, 4-1, and Wayne Gretzky suffered a back injury on a check by Suter. When you watch the NHL's greatest star go down, it makes you wonder if we should be playing a pre-season tournament.

The next game, Gary was booed by the Canadian fans, every time he touched the puck. Even Gretzky said he knew that Suter wasn't purposely trying to hurt him. We played well in Game Two. It was tied 2-2, and we had our chances. A power play gave us the opportunity to win; instead, Steve Larmer scored a shorthanded goaal with just over seven minutes left in the game. An empty-netter by Dirk Graham preserved the win.

It's too bad we couldn't have won it for Bob. At least we advanced to the finals. That's what he had asked us to do.

EPILOGUE

"I am not a prophet or a stone age man. I'm just a mortal man with potential of a Superman"
David Bowie, "Quicksand"

Scoring goals makes the hair on the back of my neck stand up. It's an incredible rush. It's an addiction; as soon as you snap the puck into the net, you immediately want to do it again so you can relive the high. The thrill is having 18,000 fans cheering so loudly that the dust is shaken from the rafters of St. Louis Arena. Just talking about it gives me goose bumps.

Pressure, tradition and loyalty are the important aspects of hockey. What I like best is having my teammates count on me for the tying goal, the go-ahead goal, the winning goal. When the game is on the line, I want the shot. I want Oatsie to send it to me for a one-timer from the left circle. Shot. Goal. *Yesssssss.*

I want it as much as Michael Jordan wants the jumper in the closing minute of the NBA final, and José Canseco wants the final swing in the seventh game of the World Series. I want the buzz of seeing the puck enter the net.

For as long as I can remember, I've felt that if I don't score a goal I've had a poor shift. If I was a coach, I would be pleased if my players had my attitude. Scoring goals is the object of the game. If it was up to me, coaches would always coach from the offensive perspective. You need grinders to win. You can't win without my kind of player. I'm not a great defensive player. But if you think you could beat a team of twenty Brett Hulls, you are sadly mistaken. Give me twenty Wayne Gretzkys and I'll beat you every time, whether Wayne ever goes in his own end or not. I'll say it again: the object of the game is to score more than the opposition.

Most coaches stress defense. But over the last twelve years, the team that has finished first or second in goals-against has won the Stanley Cup three times. The team that has finished first or second in goals-for has won the Stanley Cup eight times. I rest my case.

I've always been mystified about why some have thought I didn't have a desire to play in the NHL. When Terry Crisp used to tell me that I didn't want to play the game badly enough, I would think, *Let's see: I score goals, I love to play, I love to practice and I love to win. How can you not want a guy like me around?*

I've read stories that said I gave up on the game after I played midget in North Vancouver. I didn't give up on hockey; it gave up on me. No junior team wanted Brett Hull. I got my break in Penticton. I took advantage of it.

On one hand, I'm the encouragement for players not to give up until their last card is played. On the other hand, I'm a symbol for the many talented players who were overlooked because their desire, attitude or size didn't meet someone's subjective criteria. I wouldn't want to guess how many have gone unnoticed.

February 7, 1992 was the day the music died for Hull and Oates. We were heading for the golf course after practice that day when someone said Brian Sutter wanted to see Adam.

It was unnecessary to specify what Sutter wanted to talk to Adam about. He certainly didn't want to discuss a possible second printing of the Hull and Oates Rockin' the Blue Note poster.

Trade rumors had been dogging Adam for two months since his contract squabble had become a public debate. Sutter was obviously going to provide Oates with a new mailing address. He informed Adam he was going to the Boston Bruins in exchange for center Craig Janney and defenseman Stephane Quintal.

"I can't believe they are ruining my golf game," I said after Adam told me the news.

It was a joke to mask frustration. What I was really thinking was: "I can't believe they are ruining my life!"

Though we played together for parts of only two seasons, I viewed Oates the way Jari Kurri views Wayne Gretzky and Mike Bossy viewed Bryan Trottier. It's probably the way Gordie Howe viewed Ted Lindsay on the Red Wings. Two playing as one has been a constant theme in NHL history. When you thumb through NHL annals, high-scoring twosomes seem more prevalent than high-scoring lines. It was said Howe and Lindsay were so in tune that the center's main duty was to stay out of the way of their passes. Gretzky says he and Kurri are almost telepathic in the way they read each other's moves.

Hull and Oates had the same kind of comfort level. *Toronto Sun* sports editor Scott Morrison called us "the most dynamic and productive linemates in the NHL. Hull and Oates go together like goal and assist."

To this day, I can't believe the situation escalated to the point of Oates' banishment. My opinion is Oates might still be with the Blues had he not been bashed mercilessly by the media throughout the contract ordeal. The misery of the Oates trade was in keeping with the theme of Brett Hull's 1991-92 campaign. No one, I'll bet, has endured a more headache-riddled seventy-goal season.

It was a totally bizarre season, to say the least. It began with people criticizing me for uttering my true feelings about the Canada Cup and ended with the Blues firing Brian Sutter, the man most responsible for my development as an NHL player. In between, my general manager called me a "floater," my center and friend was traded because of a salary dispute, NHL players went on strike, and my usually durable back went out of whack.

Even my Dad took a shot at me early in the season, saying if I didn't start playing better he would have to return to being "Dennis Hull's brother."

Meanwhile, amid the turmoil, I joined Wayne Gretzky on the now two-person list of players to score seventy or more goals in three consecutive seasons. I also became the second player, after Gretzky, to score fifty goals in fifty games in two consecutive seasons. I was also the cover story for two respected non-sport publications, *The New York Times Magazine* and Canada's *Saturday Night.*

Best of times and worst of times is an accurate reading of my seventh NHL season.

At the height of the Oates trade rumors, Blues' general manager Ron Caron indicated he had talked to at least ten different teams interested in acquiring Oates. We were on a rumor-a-day pace. First, he was supposedly heading to the Los Angeles Kings for Tony Granato and Rob Blake. Then, I recall a story saying he might go to the Edmonton Oilers for Dave Manson. Next, there were reports the New York Rangers backed out of a blockbuster swap that would have sent Oates, Nelson Emerson and Jeff Brown to the Rangers for Tony Amonte, James Patrick and Darren Turcotte. Another time, he was said to be heading to the Philadelphia Flyers for Rick Tocchet and Steve Duchesne. Still another time Oates was supposed to be sent to Calgary for Doug Gilmour, a center who had played in St. Louis before being traded to the Flames.

Caron even called the New Jersey Devils to ask whether they might be interested in trading Scott Stevens back to St. Louis in a deal for Oates. Now that would have been *perfect*. We could have traded my center and good friend for a player the Blues had been forced to surrender because of a goofy ruling by an arbitrator. (Stevens was the arbitrator-ordered compensation the Devils received for the Blues' free agent signing of Brendan Shanahan.)

Meanwhile, I was attempting to mediate the Oates-Blues "peace accords." Actually, I wasn't exactly Mr. Neutrality. One day, a headline in the *St. Louis Post-Dispatch* read something like: "Hull to Blues: Pay Oates."

I regularly lobbied on Oates' behalf to whoever would listen, especially if the listeners were Blues president Jack Quinn and Caron. I also wasn't shy about letting my feelings be known to the media. "Adam just had ninety-two assists last season," I reminded everyone. "Unless you can get Wayne Gretzky or Mario Lemieux for him, there is no one you can get to replace him."

Quinn and Caron said Adam was forcing them to trade him. Adam blamed them. They blamed Adam, or his New York-based agent Lou Oppenheim. It was one of those situations that worsened every time someone opened his mouth. Just before the All-Star break in January 1992, Oppenheim said Oates would leave the Blues unless he received a new contract. In the meantime, the St. Louis sports shows started to fuel anti-Adam sentiment; he began to be booed at The Arena.

"I think a trade is inevitable," Adam said.

"Well, that's no damn good," I said, and decided to talk again to Quinn and Caron.

Truthfully, I thought Adam was worth every cent of the deal he wanted. True, the previous summer, he had agreed to a contract that would have paid him more than $3 million over four years. But after agreeing to the deal, the Hartford Whalers agreed to pay John Cullen more than $1.2 million. The Whalers aren't exactly the league spendthrifts. And other players such as Pittsburgh Penguins' Ron Francis and Montreal Canadiens' Kirk Muller crept into the $1 million range. Buffalo signed Pat LaFontaine for $1.733 million and Penguins' winger Kevin Stevens was presented with a deal for $1.375 million.

In Adam's view, his value had improved in a rapidly changing league market. And more importantly, the Blues' salary structure had changed dramatically. Because Oates was given an extension instead of a new contract, most of his money came in the final two years. He was a $1 million player at the end of his deal, but received only $420,000 last season. That ranked him fifth on the Blues' salary list behind me, Brendan Shanahan ($625,000), Garth Butcher ($600,000) and Dave Christian ($475,000). All of those players, except yours truly, joined the Blues after Oates. Christian and Shanahan were playing their first season with the Blues after signing free-agent contracts.

Oatsie told me: "I'm 29 and I'm running out of seasons. If there is money for everyone else, there's money for me. I earned it."

I agreed. But it was a difficult situation for me. First and foremost, I support my linemate and friend. On the other hand, I am beholden to Blues management for the excellent treatment I have received. I enjoy playing for the Blues and living in St. Louis. I can't imagine being anywhere else.

With that in mind, it is unfathomable why I chose to be among those opening their mouths at the wrong time. One night after Blues fans booed Oates, anger got the best of me and I ripped into the fans. It was the kind of outburst you regret almost as soon as you say it. A public apology was issued the following morning. Fans certainly have a right to their opinions and I certainly have no business criticizing Blues fans who have treated me royally since I arrived. But I wanted fans to know that I respected Adam for never quitting on the team during what had become a nasty scrap with the Blues.

Even when Oates and Caron were publicly trading volleys, Oates worked hard every shift for the Blues. He had three assists against the New Jersey Devils the night before the Blues dealt him. That says something about the man.

During an exchange of verbal blasts. Caron wounded both Adam and me with one shot. He said we were both "floaters." He said Oatsie wasn't good enough to make the Detroit Red Wings, the team Caron had fleeced to obtain Oates in one of the best trades in Blues' history.

I laughed it off as one of the ridiculous statements that comes in the heat of the battle. My attitude is, many words are said before consequences are considered. Frustration and anger can crumble a foundation of reason in a flash.

But Adam was offended. He decided to defend both of us. "I find it hard to believe that a guy who scores 160 goals over two seasons can be called a floater," he told the *St. Louis Post-Dispatch.*

Though a trade appeared inevitable, I was still hoping it could be prevented. Adam became somewhat hopeful after backing off his demands for a new contract in favor of restructuring the old deal.

Even when hope was fading, Caron met with Adam, and invited me to join in, five or six times, to discuss the entire situation. One day, I talked to Caron alone. "Look at the way he is playing," I told him. "This team needs Adam. He never left the team. He never let it down."

Caron told me it was too late. A few days later the trade was announced. "At this point, it is a relief," Oates said.

When Sutter stopped playing us on the same line in late January we knew the Hull and Oates duo was about to become history, Adam even lost his spot on the power play. The Blues and Oates were divorcing because of irreconcilable differences. The Blues retained custody of me.

Of the fifty-four goals I had at the time of the trade, Adam had assists on twenty-eight. But unlike when Peter Zezel was traded against my wishes, I didn't think I would stop scoring goals if Oates was traded. Over the past three seasons, I have developed some confidence in my ability to score—although I am still baffled by it. Together, Adam Oates and Brett Hull may be awesome. But apart, we aren't bad. I ended up scoring sixteen in my final nineteen games to reach the seventy-goal mark again.

Not bad production for a guy who had to listen to critics predict my downfall because I had only three goals after the first eight games. My second-half performance quieted the many who were acting as if I had suddenly forgotten where the net was. Most of my critics were those who tried to translate a less-than-fruitful Canada Cup participation into a poor attitude. Wrong, Very wrong.

The Canada Cup was blown way out of proportion. I wasn't bitter about the situation as much as I was disappointed by it. First, the Canada Cup is not the Stanley Cup. Sorry, I just can't get excited about it. And I would say that if I were wearing the uniform of Canada, USA or Uganda! Secondly, it was agonizing to surrender my summer for this tournament, and then not play. Against the Russians, I spent almost one full period on the bench. I played two shifts in those twenty minutes. I didn't expect special treatment. I did expect to play. It's amazingly difficult to score when your stick never leaves the bench.

The Blues never even mentioned the Canada Cup to me. Caron said later that I'm probably the kind of player who needs the summer to recuperate from a season. May be true. With my increased goal scoring came increased promotion and charity work. My summer was gone before I knew it. I certainly didn't feel refreshed by the time I showed up in St. Louis in September.

Perhaps my slow start reflected the fact I didn't have training camp with the Blues. Given the addition of several new players, I needed time to get used to playing with new faces.

Once we grew accustomed to each other, the goals started to arrive. And I started to have some fun. The more fun I have, the better I play. One stretch included a Blues-record twenty-five-game point-scoring streak. During that span, I had forty-six points and broke Bernie Federko's Blues record of eleven career hat tricks.

Heading into the January 18 All-Star game in Philadelphia, I had thirteen points in my last five games. Oates had seven points in those games. But I joked with Adam: "I get to play with you all time. I'm sick of playing with you. I want to play with Gretzky."

The line was Robitaille, Gretzky and Hull. After netting two goals and an assist, I won a new Dodge truck as the game's MVP. Playing with Gretzky was one of the highlights of my career. When I was in Los Angeles, he and wife Janet invited me to their home. They are MVP hosts. What a great couple!

Around Christmas time, I began to flirt with the fifty-in-fifty pace. I had thirty-nine goals after forty games, then forty-three after forty-two and forty-four after forty-four. Going into a five-game home stretch against Washington, Montreal, Buffalo, Los Angeles and Vancouver between January 14 and 25, I needed six goals. I scored five.

The Capitals blanked me January 14 in a 6-1 loss, then I netted a hat trick against Montreal January 16 and another goal against Buffalo January 21. In Game forty-eight against Los Angeles January 23, I scored my forty-ninth goal. Two nights later, I was shut out in an agonizing 1-0 overtime loss to Vancouver.

From there we traveled to Los Angeles for the start of a four-game road trip. It seemed rather fitting my chance at a second consecutive fifty-in-fifty campaign would come on Gretzky's home ice. This is the guy who is the standard by which all goal scorers are judged.

In the first period it didn't seem like it was going to happen. Corey Millen and Mike Donnelly were doing a thorough checking job against me. Too thorough, I thought. But that's the way goal scorers always think.

But in the second period, I got my break because for a fleeting moment Brendan Shanahan believed he was Wayne Gretzky. There was a rebound and the puck was loose in front. Shanahan, a rugged winger with a good touch, decided at that precise moment to be uncharacteristically fancy. He spun, and passed the puck back through his legs, just as I was cutting behind him. Taking the pass in stride, I didn't even look when I wristed the puck between goaltender Kelly Hrudey's pads for the fiftieth.

After the game, all Shanahan could say was "I can't believe no one got a picture of that."

I told him someday we would all get dressed up and recreate the entire play to allow a picture to be made. Problem is I don't know if he can recreate that pass. What a move! Shanahan was a tremendous acquisition for the team. Too bad we didn't end up with both him and Scott Stevens on this team.

My fifty-in-fifty shot gave rise to more talk about whether any player can top Gretzky's record of ninety-two goals in a season. Remember, Caron had predicted I might have a shot because expansion would dilute the talent pool.

At the beginning of the season, Brian Burke, my former agent, and now the general manager of the Hartford Whalers, said: "Once I saw Hank Aaron break Babe Ruth's record I decided anything was possible. Cal Ripken will probably break Lou Gehrig's record for consecutive games. And clearly, someone will get 100 goals. Is there someone now capable of doing it in the next five years? There's only one—Brett Hull. If he doesn't do it, I think you have to look at the new talent coming along."

As flattering at that statement is, I still have my doubts. Agreed, nothing is impossible. But if Wayne Gretzky couldn't top ninety-two goals, then 100 is as close to impossible as it gets. Even the addition of four more regular season games in 1992-93 only means four extra goals for a goal-per-game scorer.

Because checking is more thorough in the second half of the season, Gretzky says a person needs fifty goals in his first forty games to have a realistic shot at his mark.

My thought is it's difficult just netting fifty in fifty. And I don't care how many expansion teams are added, talent will never be diluted enough to make it an easy accomplishment. You still have to beat two defensemen and a goaltender to score. My attitude is all defensemen and goaltenders are good, or they wouldn't be in the NHL.

Perhaps the strangest game of the season came

February 13—six days after we traded Adam—when the Blues played the Bruins. Before the game, we actually had to develop a plan to shut down Adam. We approached the game like we were about to face Gretzky. In a sense, we were. Though we had marveled at Oates' playmaking ability, we have never considered how you could stop him.

"It's tough to check him or Gretzky," said Butcher. "You can't really rush them. You have to just try to contain them."

Brian Sutter decided to use Ron Wilson, Rich Sutter and Bob Bassen to check Oates. It worked. We won 4-0. The Blues are first in my thinking, but it was difficult seeing Adam get booed regularly during the game. It was unnatural thinking of him as my adversary. This is the same guy I was hanging out with a few days before. Four months after that game, I would be a member of his wedding party.

The boos started the moment Oatsie came on the ice. The only time they cheered was when he passed the puck to me during the pre-game skate. I shot and scored. Just like old times. But they began booing again when Adam was introduced as the starting center.

Adam, who admitted he was nervous about playing in front of his former home-town crowd, refused to rip the fans. "I think I played hard when I was here and I wish they would respect that," he said. "I don't think they should boo me. But my beef was never with them. I never had any animosity toward the fans. They're entitled to boo if they want."

Three nights later, Janney showed the St. Louis fans what the Blues received in exchange for Oates. He scored his second career hat trick in a 7-2 win against Calgary. Give him credit. With all of the controversy surrounding Oates' departure, it wasn't easy coming in here and replacing him.

Despite the turmoil, I did have some fun during the 1991-92 season. I had thirteen shots in one game against the Winnipeg Jets. I had 408 shots on goal, which left me six short of Dad's mark of 414 which is third on the all-time list behind Phil Esposito's 550 and 426.

I also scored once on the replay and it actually saved my point-scoring streak. With 36 seconds remaining in a New Year's Eve game against Buffalo, I scored a goal. At least I thought I did. The goal light didn't come on and the on-ice officials didn't catch it. But the replay judge was awake and credited me with the goal. Instant replay has some bugs, but it is generally a good rule. But we definitely need more cameras. There should be at least one behind every net.

An injury, the first significant one I've ever had, robbed me of seven games. Officially, it was called back spasms. More accurately, it was pulled muscles in my lower back—another unlikely occurrence in a season of many. During a March 12 home game against the Detroit Red Wings, Jeff Brown fires the puck from the blue line. Wide. Red Wings' center Steve Yzerman tries unsuccessfully to stop the puck. It takes a strange spin off his stick. I twist my body awkwardly to gain control. Pass back to the point. No pain. At least not right away. The puck is shot from the point and Ron Wilson fires it into the net for a goal. I move toward the goal. Argh! It was like someone reached into my skin and yanked every muscle.

After tests, the doctors assured me there was no serious damage. I was expected to miss only three games. A week later the back was tested with some light skating with Doug Wickenheiser and Rick Meagher. I was along the boards talking with the doctor when Wick sent me a pass from the corner. I just took a weak shot toward the goal. I repulled all the muscles. Tack on four more games on the sideline. I could have missed more had not the players' strike provided me with the opportunity for more healing time.

It was the longest lay-off I have ever had from an

injury. My dad was also rather durable throughout his career, missing only three games in his first five seasons. Call it Hull pigheadedness. When I have a pulled muscle, I don't even tell the trainer. I just figure I'll take care of it. Four years ago, my shoulder popped out during a playoff game against Chicago. I thought: How am I going to play with this? But I did. My attitude is, the more time you spend thinking about injuries, the more likely you are to get hurt.

My back didn't hurt as much as my spirit when Brian Sutter was fired after the end of the 1991-92 season. What you see as Brett Hull is what Brian Sutter has made him to be. I wasn't much of a player until Brian Sutter taught me that the definition of a winner is someone who succeeds beyond expectations, to deliver when no one thinks he or she can.

One of my shortcomings as a player was not accepting the limitations of all players. I arrived with the attitude that every player should be able to shoot, skate, stick-handle and to make certain plays at certain times.

"You have to be yourself," Brian always told me. "But you have to understand that the other twenty guys on the team are all different with different skill levels. You always have to be able to adjust your game to their game. That's what being a good player is about. You have to be patient."

Sutter always believed I should be able to play with any center and any winger. There is a perception that I was always paired with Adam since he arrived. In reality, Brian often split us up. In 1991-92, I played frequently with Ron Sutter or Ron Wilson as my center. I played on every line, except the fourth line. Tough guy Kelly Chase was even on my line a few times, though he would probably say I played on his line.

Before Brian was fired, I said it would be a mistake to get rid of him. Not long after that he was gone. Zezel. Stevens. Oates. Sutter. Do you notice every person I feel I need keeps getting shipped out?

Brian Sutter had been coach of the year just one year earlier. But after a twenty-two-point dip in the standings from the 1990-91 to 1991-92 seasons, management needed to blame someone and they chose Brian. He was unjustly carved by the media. A case in point was the acquisition of his brothers, Rich and Ron Sutter. The media ripped him for that. It was written repeatedly that other Blues resented having the coach's brothers on the team. That was absurd: you couldn't ask for two greater team players than the Sutters. There are twenty-one other teams who would gladly find room for them in their lineup.

Another inaccurate portrayal is the Blues as a divided team. After it was written once, reporters from every NHL city would come to St. Louis and ask me if there was dissension on the Blues. I kept telling them it was ridiculous, but it wouldn't die. I can tell you two things: first, any player who doesn't play doesn't like his coach. Secondly, on the Blues even the players who didn't play regularly still had the utmost respect for Brian Sutter. Just as he had as a player, Brian put all of his energy and heart into coaching.

Sutter's four-season record rivaled the best coaches. But we were 0-for-3 in the playoffs against the Chicago Blackhawks. Who's to blame? Not Brian Sutter by himself. Maybe if management had made one more trade, or one less trade, we would have beaten the Blackhawks. Maybe if the players had executed better we would have beaten the Blackhawks. That's why it's called a team game.

Apparently, other teams believed Brian Sutter was doing an excellent job because about one month after he was fired in St. Louis he was offered jobs by the expansion Ottawa Senators and the Hartford Whalers. The Los Angeles Kings and Boston Bruins also wanted to talk to him. Eventually he signed with the Boston Bruins.

Brian Sutter always prodded me to be a better leader. When Scott Stevens was ordered to the New

Jersey Devils, the Blues needed a new captain. Talk shows, fans and media raised a ruckus when Garth Butcher was named captain over me. But I had no complaints about Butcher. He's a great guy and a good friend. Perhaps Brian was just trying to tell me I had more to prove. I believed I had taken the final step toward becoming a complete player.

"Brett Hull doesn't qualify as a Lady Byng player," Caron said about me in mid-season. "He's not a killer, but he's involved enough in the traffic to get his share of penalties. There are nights when he's the complete player."

But Brian always expected more from me. He didn't even give me an "A" as alternate captain until after Adam was dealt away in February. He gave it to me when he thought I deserved it. No beef from me, because Brian Sutter is the main reason why I've led the NHL in goal scoring.

When Butcher was hurt in March, Brian had the "C" sewn on my sweater. The night I was named captain, the Blues defeated the Minnesota North Stars 5-2. I was pumped up. No coach had named me captain since I was playing youth hockey in Winnipeg. I scored the game-winning goal against the North Stars while we were shorthanded. I was flying around the ice.

Last season was also the first opportunity I had to be an NHL penalty killer. No coach had ever given me the chance. I never understood why. I also don't understand why coaches have never wanted to use me late in the game to preserve a one-goal lead. I believe that in those situations a coach should want to use players with a knack for getting and keeping the puck. If a team needs to clear the puck out of the zone, you certainly want a guy who is accustomed to defensive pressure. That would be me. Maybe I'm not considered a defensive whiz, but I certainly know how to find the puck.

But since I left Penticton, no coach has wanted to

put me out there in those situations. At Minnesota-Duluth, I never said anything about it. When I was a freshmen I was too timid. When I was a sophomore we had great penalty killers. In St. Louis, Brian would use me only in the closing seconds of a shorthanded situation. His thinking was that when the Blues player exited the penalty box we might immediately create an offensive charge.

For the last few years, I've always made a point of saying that even if I scored seventy-two, eighty-six or seventy goals in a season I couldn't compare to the NHL's great players because I didn't play in all situations like Gretzky and Pittsburgh Penguins' center Mario Lemieux or Detroit Red Wings' Steve Yzerman. I was hoping the coaches would hear that and change their minds. Every now and then, I would tell Brian I could contribute in shorthanded situations. He didn't buy it.

One day, I said to him: "Give me a chance to fail. That's all I ask. If I can't do it, then fine. You won't have me coming in here asking all the time. But let's see if I can do it before we decide I can't."

After that he started giving me ice time in short-handed situations. Mostly I think it was because he'd grown weary of my griping.

In my shorthanded debut, I swear we generated more offense than the opposing power play. No way was I going to blow this chance. After Adam was traded, my penalty-killing role increased. At season's end, I had five shorthanded goals. Only Yzerman, with eight, had more. And our penalty killing didn't exactly go downhill. We finished fifth in the league with an 83.5 percent efficiency.

The most dramatic goal I ever scored also came in 1991-92 during a double-overtime playoff thriller against the Chicago Blackhawks. It was a great game with great goaltending. When it was over, Blues goaltender Curtis Joseph and Chicago's Dominik Hasek had faced a collective total of 76 shots. Both goaltenders were awesome in the overtime.

In the first overtime, Hasek stopped one of my snap shots from the right circle. I gained control of the rebound, came around the back of the net to the left circle, and fired a hard shot right into his chest.

Meanwhile, Joseph stopped Brian Noonan on a breakaway.

Later, I made a rare end-to-end rush, beat the defenseman, only to have Hasek slide in front of a wrister to thwart my breakaway.

It was a weird feeling playing that kind of game. Every chance the Blackhawks had, I would be thinking "Oh, Oh" and then someone would stop them. I would say: "Thank God, they didn't score." Then, we would blow a chance. And I'm thinking, "Oh, no, we didn't score." It was an emotionally draining contest.

Finally, we cashed in on a chance early in the second overtime. Ron Sutter sent a pass to Bob Bassen at the Chicago blue line. He dropped the puck for me in the high slot, about 30 feet away from the net. Chicago defenseman Steve Smith was in front of me, but he was trying to move away to give Hasek a chance to see the puck. I waited for him to clear, because I didn't want it blocked. I beat Hasek cleanly at 3:33.

Apparently my Dad predicted before the overtime to Blues chairman Mike Shanahan that I would score the overtime goal. Afterward, reporters asked me whether I thought I was going to score.

Of course I did. "Every single guy wanted to score. If he didn't he shouldn't be out there," I said.

The next day, the headline in the paper was: "Hull's Called Shot Strikes Out Hawks."

Unfortunately, it turned out to be a meaningless goal because the Blackhawks knocked us out of the playoffs.

I was envious watching the Pittsburgh Penguins win their second consecutive Stanley Cup. Penguins' general manager Craig Patrick has done a masterful job of acquiring the right people to complete a championship team. Obtaining Ron Francis in 1990-91 and then Rick Tocchet in 1991-92? That's great management. I'm wondering what those other teams were thinking about when they traded those guys to the Penguins. It's like conceding the Cup to Pittsburgh.

Patrick had four or five great offensive players, then went out and found eight great big defensemen. They are space eaters who can shoot, skate and hit. When you play the Penguins, you always feel as if there is no room in the offensive zone. You can get claustrophobic just crossing their blue line. It seems as if their defensemen are all seven feet tall. Every time you look up, you see this big, black Penguin coming right at you.

And their power play? Mario Lemieux, Kevin Stevens, Joe Mullen, Jaromir Jagr, Francis and Tocchet. It's just scary.

Another thing: Lemieux never gets enough credit. He keeps doing it every season, but there always seem to be questions about him. I recall everyone predicting he would never play after his back surgery. Two Stanley Cups later he is still in the lineup and he looks like he's still having fun.

To my mind, that's the key to success in any sport. I stopped worrying about losing Adam Oates the day he left. Someday, he and I might talk about the "what ifs," but right now I only worry about what is. I still like the St. Louis Blues' organization. I enjoy my teammates. I like Chase dragging me, against my better judgment, to listen to country music. I like the fact that Garth Butcher helped me find my dream car—the 1957 Porsche Speedster. I like to see Bob Goodenow, my former agent, unifying the players' association. He was Gretzky-like in his performance during the players strike.

I like Bob Berry giving me grief every minute of every day. One of the more positive aspects of the changing Blues organization has been Berry's promotion to assistant general manager. Who knows how it will unfold, but he appears in line to replace Caron when he retires in a couple of years.

I don't have time to worry about losing Adam because I'm busy worrying about trying to win the Stanley Cup. If you can't accept change, you can't enjoy life. Besides, if you spend too much time fretting about your lost Oates, the giant Penguins will eat you alive.

**Great Sports Titles
from M&S Paperbacks...**

BRETT
by Brett Hull and Kevin Allen
The NHL's most prolific goal-scorer, son of the great Bobby Hull, chronicles his own rise to hockey superstardom in this revealing autobiography.
0-7710-4271-X $6.99   24 pages b&w photos

THE HABS
An Oral History of the Montreal Canadiens: 1940-1980
by Dick Irvin
"A beautiful read." — *Hockey News*
"A wealth of hockey lore." — *The Toronto Star*
Veteran broadcaster Dick Irvin presents the vivid stories of more than one hundred players, coaches, officials and journalists as they recall the glory days of Canada's most successful sports franchise.
0-7710-4358-9 $6.99   16 pages b&w photos

SITTLER
by Darryl Sittler and Chrys Goyens with Allan Turowetz
"Sittler tells his story the way he played — bluntly and bravely." — Jim Proudfoot, *The Toronto Star*
Few Toronto Maple Leafs have been as beloved or respected as Hockey Hall-of-Famer Darryl Sittler. Here he provides an honest, occasionally painful look at his 15-season career in Canada's national sport.
0-7710-8080-8 $6.99   16 pages b&w photos